To Be Or Not To Be

DUNCAN WILLIAMS

To Be Or Not To Be

———◆———

A Question of Survival

———◆———

DAVIS-POYNTER
LONDON

First published in 1974 by
Davis-Poynter Limited
20 Garrick Street London WC2E 9BJ

Copyright © 1974 by Duncan Williams

ISBN 0 7067 0133 X

The author and publishers are grateful for permission to quote from the following :
Joseph Wood Krutch, *The Modern Temper*, Harcourt Brace Jovanovich Inc. New York, 1930; Alvin Toffler, *Future-Shock*, The Bodley Head Ltd, 1970; and to The Society of Authors for permission to quote from *Too True To Be Good* by George Bernard Shaw. In addition, the author has drawn on a large number of other works, the majority of which are listed in the Bibliography.

Printed in Great Britain by
Bristol Typesetting Co. Ltd
Barton Manor St Philips Bristol

For my wife, Pam,
whose devotion and loyalty
have encouraged and sustained me
through all my endeavours.

CONTENTS

———————◆———————

INTRODUCTION   *page* 9

   I   The Problem   15

  II Change and Progress   29

 III Knowledge and Wisdom   37

 IV Supra-culture and Anarchy   48

   V High Living and Plain Thinking   59

 VI Education for What?   68

 VII Rediscovery   79

VIII Contemporary Idols of the Cave   94

 IX Is Man Worth Saving?   118

EPILOGUE   139

SELECTED BIBLIOGRAPHY   151

INDEX   155

INTRODUCTION

It may well be that unconsciously the seeds of a new book are contained in the author's previous one, although when the manuscript of *Trousered Apes* was completed some years ago and the last chapter entitled 'To Be Or Not To Be', I had no knowledge or premonition that the genesis of the present volume was contained therein. It soon became apparent, however, that although *Trousered Apes* had, to my satisfaction at least, *diagnosed* some of the problems besetting contemporary man, it was stunted and incomplete because it failed to provide any prescription for a cure to these same ills. A former student of mine, reviewing the book in an American journal, after a generally laudatory notice, spotlighted this deficiency when he concluded : 'Once the problems have been delineated and the failings of orthodox thought have been exposed, the author tends to adopt a hortary tone in an effort to avoid revealing his lack of convincing solutions.'

I cannot judge whether or not the solutions outlined in this book are 'convincing', but it is an honest attempt to provide such a prescription (and like most medicine will prove unpalatable to many); to that extent it should be seen as a complement to, and an extension of, the views expressed in *Trousered Apes*.

It has long been apparent to me that with one or two notable exceptions, such as G. Rattray Taylor's *Rethink,* Hugh Montefiore's *Can Man Survive?* or Wynne-Tyson's *The Civilised Alternative,* the field of environmental studies has been dominated either by highly technical writers whose message is confined to fellow-specialists, or by those whose passionate feelings on ecology have only been matched by their reluctance to arrive at the logical conclusions to their own arguments. *To Be Or Not To Be* is a modest attempt to redress the balance.

The statistical and technical evidence of mankind's present predicament is, so far as possible, confined to the opening chapter, and the remainder of the book is devoted to an

A*

analysis of these problems together with certain suggested remedies. The latter are presented from a cultural and educational stand-point and although in a book of this length they must be of a somewhat general nature, I have nevertheless attempted to be specific in certain areas, content to leave the wider application to the acknowledged experts.

If this book has a central message it must be that unregenerate men and women, devoid of awe and reverence, no matter how expert their technology, or how superficially sophisticated and plausible their arguments and opinions may seem, cannot do anything other than hasten the decline and fall of mankind. Governments of all political persuasions in all countries are being impelled by 'popular' but unthinking demands either to embark upon, or to persist in, policies and actions which are Gadarene in destination; God or 'The Great First Cause' may not be conservative, but he is most certainly a conservationist, and Nature, his *locum tenens* on earth, is rapidly cashing collective man's reckless and extravagant cheques. Unless we speedily adopt a more humble and prudent attitude, individually and societally, we will be ecologically and spiritually bankrupt and the receivers, in the shape of famine, pestilence and nihilism, will take possession. Whatever the faults of organized religion (and they were manifest and manifold) it did inculcate in centuries past, throughout a large section of society, a spirit of reverence and humility; the absence of these two qualities, no matter how 'beneficial' in social, educational, cultural and materialistic terms, has nonetheless inexorably brought the human species to what Arnold Toynbee calls 'the eleventh hour', not just of civilization but of survival.

The late Evelyn Waugh wrote to the Conservative Prime Minister of the day, protesting that although he (Waugh) had voted Conservative throughout his life, successive governments had 'failed to put the clock back one second'. Although this book is apolitical (indeed in intent anti-political) people of all political persuasions are beginning to perceive that environmentally the clock must, at least temporarily, be stopped if not put into reverse.

If the title 'reactionary' implies a person who wishes to return to the less frenzied, less cut-throat society – one in which a sense of community and of 'belonging' supersedes the cheap thrills, sensationalism and faceless anonymity of megalopolitan life – then I claim such a title with pride. Again, with those who would accuse me of chauvinism or nationalism I obligingly concur. Internationalism, physically manifest in slab, uniform, dreary architecture is already with us, 'decorating' almost every airport and ancillary building in the world and busily extending its domination of skylines from Sydney to San Francisco. Socially and culturally the process is only a step or two behind, as witness the increasing uniformity of the 'youth culture', with its mid-Atlantic 'newspeak', discothèque music, which permeates all national boundaries and bogus 'folk' art – the latter a billion-dollar industry based in Memphis, Tennessee.

There are, too, the international nature and attitudes of such disparate organizations as industrial and commercial conglomerates, the metrication and decimalization boards, societies for safeguarding universal human rights (but never, curiously, for the proclamation of human duties) world trades-unionism, church ecumenicalism, television and film media which transmit stereotyped 'sophisticated' pseudo-violence amid an equally pseudo-geographical locale. All of these powerful movements are designed, consciously or unconsciously, to destroy, or render obsolete, peculiarities and above all *differences* in human nature, institutions and *mores*. Yet one must be a cultural peasant if one fails to recognize that variety is not only the spice of life but the very stuff out of which life is made, and a world in which nothing but the temperature and climate allowed one to know whether one was in Cairo or Cincinnati, London or Las Palmas, would surely prove infinitely 'weary, stale, flat, and unprofitable'. Presenting, as it will, unless challenged, a social and psychological version of what geologists refer to as a peneplain – an almost totally flat, featureless landscape – it is extremely doubtful whether such an environment would provide a *milieu* in which the individual and collective human spirit (with the exception of totally insensitive profiteers or narcissistic demagogues) could either flourish or indeed desire to do so. Decades hence a future Blake may coin the apothegm: 'What now is acknowledg'd Truth, was once dismiss'd as mere Prejudice.'

There is a small tablet in St Paul's Cathedral commemorating the achievement of Sir Christopher Wren. Very simply it states: *si monumentum requiris circumspice* (If you would see his monument, look around). It might be salutary for all teachers, myself included, who feel that they have performed their task sufficiently when their charges are able to read, write and calculate, speak French or Spanish fluently and accurately, or have mastered the abstractions of advanced mathematics or analytical logic, to be taken out into the streets of London, Chicago or Rome to see the hideous and brutalizing 'monumental' hen-coops which planners, politicians, builders and architects – the privileged recipients of mere literacy and numeracy divorced from any ethical or aesthetic sensibility – are erecting as accommodation for their fellow humans.

Finally I must confess that many nights during the writing of this book I have lain awake plagued by doubts and uncertainties as to the wisdom of including certain thoughts and passages. On such occasions the mocking lines of Pope have frequently haunted my mind :

> Truths would you teach, or save a sinking land?
> All fear, none aid you and few understand.
> Painful pre-eminence! yourself to view
> Above life's weakness, and its comforts too.

I can only hope that after reading the book, *many* will at least understand my motives in writing it and that *few* will fear its overall message.

Although none of the following of necessity shares my views, I must not fail to record my indebtedness and gratitude to them : firstly to Hugh Montefiore, Bishop of Kingston, for permission to reproduce *A New Decalogue*, which was originally part of his Rutherford Lecture of 1972. He has asked me to stress that this decalogue is emphatically *not* to be construed as supplanting the Ten Commandments but is to be viewed only as supplementary to them; secondly to the President and Tutors of St John's College, Maryland, USA for permission to include details of their unique and highly successful undergraduate curriculum. I am also most grateful to the following : Gordon Rattray Taylor, author of *The Biological Time Bomb, Rethink,* and other seminal books, for permission to reproduce the table at the foot of page 49; and Mr. Yehudi Menuhin for allowing me to quote from a letter on page 19.

I should also like to express my gratitude to the Council of the Farmington Trust for whom a pamphlet was written out of which this book has grown. Finally and particularly I wish to thank the Hon. Robert Wills, whose generosity and encouragement have made it possible; my colleague Mr. Edward Hulmes, who read the book in manuscript and made several invaluable comments and suggestions; and Mrs. Pamela Stone, who has uncomplainingly and indeed, with at least an appearance of cheerfulness, typed and re-typed the manuscript.

DUNCAN WILLIAMS

A NEW DECALOGUE
by
THE RT. REV. HUGH MONTEFIORE, BISHOP OF KINGSTON
(Rutherford Lecture, London 1972)

1. I am the Lord your God. You shall have no other God but me.

2. You shall not make for yourself any graven image or idol such as the Gross National Product or possessions or riches. You shall not bow down and serve them.

3. You shall not take the name of the Lord your God in vain, by calling on His name but ignoring His natural law.

4. Remember that you set apart one day in the week for true festivity, or you will be bored stiff in the technological age you are bringing on yourselves.

5. Honour your father and your mother, but do not seek to prolong their natural life so that they are miserable.

6. You shall not murder future generations by your present greed.

7. You shall not commit sexual sin by producing more children than is your right.

8. You shall not steal the inheritance of posterity.

9. You shall not bear false witness against your overseas neighbours, by lying to yourself about the extent of their need.

10. You shall not covet an ever-increasing standard of living.

CHAPTER I

The Problem

———◆———

Most of us are private citizens, who can only do little
things. But the whole world is made up of private
citizens, and if they can see the situation, then the
situation may be changed.
C. P. SNOW: 'The State of Siege', Westminster College,
Missouri, 1968

———◆———

As the human race increases in numbers but not perceptibly in intelligence or that indefinable quality which we
call wisdom, so the problems, complexities and frustrations of
ordinary existence multiply and threaten to reach overwhelming proportions in the decades ahead. Indeed, as one
looks forward, one is reminded of Adlai Stevenson who,
having visited Los Angeles, is said to have remarked on his
return : 'I have seen the future and it doesn't work.'

Only a few years ago, this would have seemed an eccentric
minority view, but far too many eminent men and women
are today questioning the basic assumptions of a society
increasingly characterized by over-population, civil strife,
pollution, urban blight and neuroses, strikes, gross materialism, exploitation and inflation, for those concerned to be
designated as mere cranks. A highly intelligent undergraduate
appeared to speak for a sizeable number of her generation
when she remarked a year or two ago : 'The past is irrelevant
and the future unthinkable.'

The *physical* effects of a geometrically-escalating population
are already everywhere in evidence – overcrowded schools,
cities, highways, beaches, prisons, airports, hospitals – the list
is endless, and one might cynically anticipate that the children
of today's demonstrators may in the 1980's shoulder banners
proclaiming the message : 'Make *War* Not Love'. (The
curious phenomena of the 'Manson cult', Hell's Angels and
the Theatre of Cruelty, are in their different ways surely

significant omens.) Moreover, historically speaking, there is
little reason to assume that the next generation will not
accuse *its* parents of stupidity or myopia in much the same
way as do today's youthful radicals. Alexander Pope's observation in 1711 is still devastatingly true :

> We think our fathers fools, so wise we grow;
> Our wiser sons, no doubt, will think us so.

In the particular case of the population problem, one
cannot escape the hard, uncomfortable fact that isolated
individuals have been attempting for centuries to forewarn
a largely indifferent public of this menace. Thomas Malthus
realized the danger as long ago as 1798, but until comparatively recently a blind faith in what might be styled loosely
'agricultural technology' caused all but a perceptive few to
deny the validity of his logic and to indulge in melioristic
fantasies.[1]

Lately, however, some influential voices have adopted a
more Malthusian view. In 1956 Julian Huxley, who was then
Secretary General of UNESCO, declared that if nothing were
done to control population, mankind would become 'the
cancer of the planet and drown in its own flood.'

In November 1968 Lord Snow delivered an address at
Westminster College, Missouri in which he envisioned in the
near future an almost inevitable collision between the rapidly
increasing world population and the means of producing
sufficient food to avert famine on an unprecedented global
scale :

> In many places and for many purposes, including some of
> the fundamental human purposes, there are already too
> many people in the world. Within a generation, there will
> be far too many. Within two or three generations – unless
> we show more sense, goodwill and foresight than men
> have ever shown – there will be tragically too many. So
> many that the ordinary human hopes will have disappeared.

---

[1] The following by Wordsworth in the Preface to the second edition
of *Lyrical Ballads* (1800) has, despite its somewhat archaic language,
a distinctly modern ring. He speaks of 'a multitude of causes, unknown
to former times which are now acting with a combined force to
blunt the discriminating powers of the mind . . . to reduce it to a
state of almost savage torpor.' Among these causes he lists 'the increasing accumulation of men in cities, where the uniformity of their occupa-
tions produces a craving for extraordinary incident which the rapid
communication of intelligence hourly gratifies.'

Professor Paul Ehrlich's *The Population Bomb* expresses an even more pessimistic view.

Most demographers and agricultural experts acknowledge the existence of the problems, but both parties tend to ask the other for breathing space. The demographers acknowledge that there is no method of curtailing population growth within ten years and call on the agronomists to produce some 'super-grain' to tide them over these years. The agronomists make the same sort of demands in reverse. The problem is, of course, further accentuated by the fact that the 'underdeveloped' nations of the world, through television and films, are now seeing, in many cases for the first time, what the 'haves' have. (I can remember watching a light-hearted American comedy in Mombasa some twenty years ago. The audience, predominantly African and Arab, while amused at the antics of the suburban couple, were even more impressed with the two-car garages, refrigerator and all the other appurtenances of what is almost universally conceived to be an average American home.) To expect these people to remain docile and quiescent in the face of such tempting vision is to ignore what Samuel Johnson called 'that hunger of the imagination which preys incessantly upon life.'

The social philosopher may reflect ironically that such aspirations, when realized, will result in what F. R. Leavis has dismissed as 'the empty world of swimming pools and sports cars, of triumphant technology and high standards of living coupled with life-impoverishment and human emptiness' – the very world in fact that a growing proportion of affluent Western youth (as symbolized in the film, *The Graduate*) is so loudly rejecting.

Such sophisticated reasoning is impossible to the Tanzanian peasant or any other inhabitant of the Third World. To persuade him that perhaps an underdeveloped country offers more cultural diversity, spiritual fulfilment and contentment than an over-developed one would be futile and possibly dangerous.

Moreover, the pious wish that these countries may 'catch up with us' is rather like hoping that a pedestrian progressing at four miles an hour may overtake an automobile travelling at sixty. (The fact that the motorist in his haste may be heading towards a precipice seems to be beside the point.) The 'pedestrian' now knows, vicariously, the joys of 'motoring' and is demanding an 'automobile' for himself. Due to his ever-increasing numbers, however, his anxious government is pondering the problem of keeping him even decently 'shod'.

Lest I be accused of sentimentalizing over the contentment of primitive peoples perhaps I ought to remark, parenthetically, that I lived in East Africa for a period of more than three years, mostly in the bush.

On those rare occasions when I did visit Nairobi or any other city I was invariably struck by the strained 'commuter' expressions on the faces of the urbanized Africans compared with the relaxed, if slightly indolent, lives of their rural counterparts. More recently I spent a year in a remote Oxfordshire village which had been spared the more extreme ravages of twentieth-century life. Again there was this *contentment* among the villagers grouped around the fireside in the pub in the evenings – a contentment which correctly or not I attributed to the seasonal rhythm of their lives and the obvious justification for their existence in the raising of food for their families and the community – a justification which modern industrial life, symbolized by the conveyor belt, appears incapable of providing for any but the totally unimaginative and insensitive. I am not in any way advocating a Rousseauistic 'Noble Savage' solution to contemporary ills and certainly do not wish to ignore the infinitely superior health and educational facilities which cities offer. But a good physique and sophisticated learning may be at least questionable substitutes for peace of mind.

Moreover, from a global perspective it would be utterly disastrous were the materialistic standards of the overdeveloped nations to spread uniformly from country to country. If the present level of American industrialization, electrification, transportation, and so forth became a basic norm, a *very* brief period of prosperity would ensue, but the earth would become speedily uninhabitable. The dissemination of the 'American way of life' would mean that the earth's atmosphere would have to absorb 200 times more sulphur dioxide and trioxide than it does now; 750 times more carbon monoxide, dioxide and benzopyrene; 10,000 times more asbestos. More than thirty million acres of arable land would be swallowed up annually to make way for cities, highways, airports and other transit systems.[2] Obviously, this

---

[2] I am indebted for these figures to an editorial by Norman Cousins in the *Saturday Review* (June 20, 1970).

cannot happen without creating eco-catastrophe, but what will? A global solution is needed and a sense of human responsibility to match this awesome problem. At the moment there is no lack of generous-minded people whose energies are enlisted to champion various causes, but these are always invariably factional and consequently divisive. As Yehudi Menuhin recently wrote in a letter :

> Any narrowing of the broader motive carries with it the need to act against the particular, in other words against the remainder. If one does not include in some way the whole of living existence on our planet in one's basic attitudes and morality, one finds oneself acting on behalf of one part against the other. . . . There is today no lack of people ready to discipline themselves and sacrifice themselves, but the mistake is that this eternal capacity for self-immolation (along with the immolation of others) is held at the service of partisan causes exclusively, fought with enormous dedication and courage, but almost never on behalf of the enemy or of life in general. The desire to improve oneself materially, and the false spiritual justification employed, seems almost always tied up with the compulsion to destroy others, and the same goes hand in hand with the desire to enjoy, to assert or to castigate. Man can no longer afford to act so blindly today, without bringing desolation on the whole planet. Therefore we must learn to fight for total life and total survival, and against all immediate baser and partisan ends.
>
> If through our folly, we continue on our present march towards self-extermination, then man will have no one but himself to blame, and it will not matter very much who presides over the final extermination — fascist, communist, Black Panther, Weathermen, IRA — for there will be no one left to record it and the ultimate Pyrrhic victory by man over man will have been achieved.

So far I have referred only to the physical and quantitatively measurable aspects of the population problem, and it is essential to realize that the human race is adding to its numbers the equivalent of the inhabitants of a large city, more than 195,000 people, *every day of the week,* of which number rather more than three-quarters are being added to the poorer nations.[3] Less obvious, and therefore potentially

---

[3] This figure, obtained from the *Demographic Year Book, 1970,* United Nations, New York 1971, p. 105, takes into account deaths and stillbirths and refers exclusively to the total net increase per day.

much more dangerous, are the psychological symptoms of overpopulation.

Stephen Spender has recalled that in 1930 he asked the late T. S. Eliot what future he (Eliot) foresaw for our civilization. Eliot's reply, in the light of recent events, appears unpleasantly prophetic : 'Internecine fighting . . . People killing one another off in the streets.'

From an examination of other species in overcrowded conditions we know that such overcrowding results in a form of mass-psychosis. Previously docile creatures attack and kill one another *even though* provided with an abundance of food.[4] The most recent experiment with mice in the United States paints an even gloomier picture. In a five-year experiment begun in 1968 a colony of mice was provided with all the necessary ingredients for a long and happy life – food, drink, comfortable conditions, protection from the elements, and no external stresses. In slightly less than five years it had died out completely. When the total population reached 150 all the available space was filled, mothers chased their young out of the nests and the dominant males suffered something tantamount to a breakdown. This was accompanied by female aggressiveness and domination and, despite their physical well-being, the mice lost interest both in courtship and mating. When the population reached 2,200 breeding ceased entirely, the last mouse dying in January 1973. The report of this experiment suggests that there is no logical reason why a comparable sequence of events should not also lead to the extinction of mankind.[5]

Although it is notoriously dangerous to draw comparisons between human beings and other species, there appears to be no valid reason to assume that man is an exception to this phenomenon, and it is surely significant that mass, often irrational violence most frequently occurs in those areas where overcrowding and slums conspire to bring about conditions parallel to those used in experiments with animals. Under these circumstances it must be a case of crass abdication of responsibility for 'pop' art to aid, however slightly, in making urban blight and ugliness a norm instead of opposing

---

[4] 'Population Density and Social Pathology', J. B. Calhoun, M.D., *Scientific American,* February, 1962, Vol. 206, 2, pp. 139–148.
[5] *'Death Squared'*, J. B. Calhoun, M.D., *Proc. Roy. Soc. Med.* Vol. 66, January 1973.

such and offering alternatives based on beauty and order,
towards which contemporary man can at least aspire. Even
more alarming and sinister is the tendency to label concern
for the appearance of cities and indeed concern for the environment itself as 'bourgeois', or even racist, thereby creating
the delusion that this is merely another element of class warfare when obviously, if man is to survive, it must become a
universal concern.

Certain radical theologians, too, in their 'deterministic'
pragmatism must share some of the guilt. Harvey Cox, for
example, in *The Secular City*, appears to see in modern urban
society with all its concomitant evils and distresses and its
purely secular attitudes, a manifestation of the will of God.[6]
'All idols and icons *must* be exposed, for the relative, con-
ditional things they are. Tribal (rural) naïveté *must* be laid
to rest everywhere and everyone *must* be made a citizen of the
land of broken symbols.'[7] (The italics are, of course, mine and
illustrate the essentially totalitarian thought-processes and
iconoclasm of much of Cox's thesis.) What is not clear is what
one does after we have all become citizens of his 'Waste Land'.
Certainly there is no room here for 'that peace of mind which
passeth all understanding'. On the contrary, he declares in an
almost insanely optimistic fashion that 'the fact that urban-
secular man is incurably and irreversibly pragmatic, that he
is less and less concerned with religious questions, is in no
sense a disaster. It means that he is shedding the lifeless
cuticles of the mythical and ontological period and stepping
into the *functional* age.'[8] Elsewhere he suggests that the doctrines of the present-day Church derive from the 'frayed-out
period of classical Christendom and are infected with the
ideology of preservation and permanence.' The sentiments inherent in the foregoing are totally opposed to the *cumulative*
wisdom of mankind and to what one instinctively knows to
be true – that without some sense of permanency, however

---

[6] It is interesting to compare Cox's theory with the words of Thomas
Jefferson: 'I view great cities as pestilential to the morals, the health
and the liberties of man.' Even a cursory glance at megalopolitan life
compared with that of a village, will reveal that if Cox is correct,
then we are at the mercy of a malevolent deity compared with whom
Hardy's 'President of the Immortals', who had 'ended his sport with
Tess', is a pleasantly avuncular figure.
[7] Macmillan New York, 1966, pp. 34–5.
[8] *Ibid*, p. 69.

illusory, both individual man and collective society are doomed to fragmentation and eventual social, political and spiritual anarchy.

Indeed, a comparison between a newspaper or television news-programme of today with one of even ten years ago might suggest that there are already apparent, ominous signs of incipient world anarchy – that state which W. B. Yeats dreaded and to which, half a century ago, he gave prophetic utterance :

> Things fall apart; the centre cannot hold . . .
> The blood-dimmed tide is loosed, and everywhere
> The ceremony of innocence is drowned.

Although we have yet to devise an instrument capable of measuring the psychic temperature of a generation or of any particular historical epoch, the spectacle of ever-growing numbers, increasingly demanding equal shares in a world in which, relatively speaking, space, food and consequently the opportunity to live a life of human dignity and significance are all rapidly diminishing, would seem to dictate a period of total and unrelieved strife in the years ahead.

In short, we have learnt to 'control' death but have failed, on a global scale, to 'control' birth.[9] (One has only to visit a beach almost anywhere on the British or North American coasts on a summer day and speculate where all the children – happily swimming, paddling, or building sandcastles – will park *their* cars or for that matter, themselves, when they reach maturity, to realize the full magnitude of the problem, even in these countries, let alone in South America, Africa and Asia.)

---

[9] 'Vast famines are now quite inevitable in the underdeveloped countries within the next ten years. These will have their repercussions in making our food imports scarcer and more expensive. Our farming is already too intensive for indefinite maintenance, our soil is steadily deteriorating owing to excessive use of chemical fertilizers – in fact we are living off our soil capital . . . It is now time for the country to realise that it is not feasible for the Government and doctors to interfere with nature's population control by instituting death-control, without at the same time ensuring that births are correspondingly controlled.' Dr. P. N. Edmunds, M.D. in a letter to the *Daily Telegraph,* January 13, 1972. Even as I write this, over a year later, escalating food prices are already a major fact of life and cause for concern among ordinary housewives, who unfortunately, for the most part, are unaware of the real source of their growing discontent.

The situation is further aggravated by the fact that politicians, trade-unionists and other leaders throughout the world get elected, and retain power, by increasing the materialistic aspirations of the electorates, and even in Communist countries such as the USSR, rising affluence has, inevitably, been accompanied by rising effluence. If religion was formerly, as Marx asserted, 'the opium of the people', politics as presently conceived and executed, has become the heroin of the twentieth century; peoples, the world over, are being induced to demand a *higher* standard of living when survival of the entire species is predicated on a revolution of *declining* materialistic expectations.

In the case of overcrowding among animals (even docile ones) to which I referred previously, through the process which was described as mass-psychosis but which more specifically involves a combination of cannibalism and homosexuality, the creatures gradually reduce their numbers to a tolerable level, and even exterminate themselves.

I trust that I will not be accused of being excessively morbid and speculative in suggesting that latent cannibalism may be detected in many areas of contemporary life – the generation conflict; the growing hostility between the sexes; the racial situation in the United States and elsewhere; the Sino-Russian conflict; the Ulster situation and many others. All these are symptomatic of a society increasingly characterized by fragmentation at a time when more than ever before cohesion should be a basic and undisputed goal.

(As a grim parenthesis, I can vividly remember the American 'youth-leader', Jerry Rubin, telling a wildly cheering crowd of young people on the campus of Kent State University to 'go home and kill your parents'.) And is not the modish cult of unisex merely another manifestation of this same crisis? That this cannot be proved empirically is undeniable but no one, for example, could have *proved* in 1780 that the French Revolution would occur nine years later although, with the gift of hindsight, present-day historians can see the combination of circumstances which led, seemingly inexorably, to that event.

As I have suggested elsewhere,[10] a number of logs floating

---

10 *Trousered Apes*. Churchill Press (London, 1971); Arlington House (New Rochelle, 1972).

on the surface of a river may point in apparently random directions; some will point down-stream, some horizontally to the banks, others at varying angles. The casual observer might regard them as being totally directionless pieces of timber, but a penetrating eye discerns that in spite of their divergent positions they are all being borne in one direction by the current. At times they move with great rapidity; at others the movement may be so slow as to be almost unobservable.

This phenomenon has a parallel in the *Zeitgeist,* that is in the intellectual and moral tendencies of an age. Beneath the surface there is a current, a predominating trend and although it may be more difficult to discern in one's own age than in those of the past it need not therefore be invisible. One thing *is* certain and that is that we need a sane and comprehensive world population plan far more than most people realize. And we need it *soon.* Mankind inherited a fair world with the possibility of a sufficiency of food (in the form of both meat for the hunter and of soil capable of nurturing the seed for the farmer), water and the necessary wood and stone to provide shelter. The foregoing is axiomatic since the whole evolutionary theory rests on the premise that natural conditions must exist and be *right* for a species to emerge and then endure. We have, however, increasingly exhibited a reckless lack of husbandry which, were it applied to a microcosm (for example, an individual farm), would speedily result in the farmer's bankruptcy and total ruin of the land. Complete pragmatism, shorn of any principle, is directly contrary to Nature which exhibits certain *constant* and *enduring* rules. Moreover, we have never seriously attempted to produce good 'husbandmen' – Plato's concept of Philosopher-Kings remains just that, a concept and no more. (As Sir Richard Livingstone observed in *Some Tasks For Education* : 'It is not surprising that human character has not improved, for we have never taken its improvement seriously in hand.'[11])

Politicians, whose business is, after all, to obtain votes, must appear to be interested only in the good and happiness of the individual 'animals' and not in the health and solvency of the 'farm'.

If we are to recognize what Alexander Pope in the *Essay*

---

[11] Toronto, 1946, p. 28.

on Man called 'self-love' (i.e. the appetitive element in human nature) as a constant, then we should seek to inculcate 'reason, to restrain' as a vital balancing factor. As the economist Kenneth Boulding has written: 'We are all guilty of ignorance, frivolity and blindness and the accusing fingers of billions of the unborn are pointed angrily towards us.'[12] (The American comic strip, *Peanuts*, expresses it even more pointedly: 'We have recognized the enemy and it is US').

What we are in danger of ignoring or forgetting, however, is that the so-called 'population explosion' is in fact a direct product of the unchecked and accelerating growth of technology which is appearing more and more in the guise of a Frankenstein monster, created by what the American anthropologist, Loren Eiseley, has aptly called 'that completely amateur sorcerer – man'.

In consequence, never before in recorded history has the human species been confronted with the necessity to adapt and to change its basic ideas, beliefs, prejudices and modes of life so radically as today. At the same time never have so many spectres haunted the minds of sensitive, thoughtful men and women.

In addition to the ominous rise in world-population, one might cite the following: age-old national rivalries, coupled with racial tension and violence which carry within them the seeds of the destruction of civilization itself; the nuclear ability of man to exterminate himself and all other life; the knowledge explosion, entailing either a forced, narrow, desiccated specialization or, alternatively, an intellectual frustration as a diminishing few vainly attempt to sustain the old, humanistic renaissance ideal[13]; the youthful rebellion which, however idealistic in origin, betrays only too often the basic and fatal flaw of the quixotic revolutionary – action divorced from thought, intelligence without wisdom, destruction for

---

[12] *The Meaning of the Twentieth Century* (London, 1964) p. 135.
[13] The total world output of books alone is approaching the prodigious figure of *one thousand titles per day*. Moreover, the United States Government *alone* is responsible for issuing 100,000 reports in the course of a year together with 450,000 articles, books and papers. (I am indebted to Alvin Toffler's *Future Shock* for this information.) Meanwhile the *News of the World* consumes over three-quarters of a million trees annually to provide itself with paper to chronicle the more dismal and disillusioning actions and aspects of *homo sapiens*.

its own sake; the growing inability of many educated minds to find consolation in assurances of an after-life; and finally, the rapid erosion (if not total disappearance) of traditional ethical and moral standards. As Aldous Huxley, wrote, shortly before his death in 1963:

> It is against this background of chronic upheaval that the members of a species, biologically and historically adapted to a slowly changing environment must now live out their bewildered lives.[14]

It is interesting to ponder the implications of Huxley's words and to compare his attitude with that of Harvey Cox and also of Alvin Toffler. In *Future Shock* the latter, after describing the nineteenth century's glorification of 'home' as 'syrupy', proceeds to stigmatize the following lines by Tennyson as 'classically cloying':

> An English home – gray twilight poured
> On dewy pastures, dewy trees,
> Softer than sleep – all things in order stored,
> A haunt of ancient peace.
> [*The Palace of Art*, 85–88]

Is it, one wonders, an impatience with order, restraint and harmony that causes both writers to attack the classical tradition, or are they themselves so infected by the virus of innovation that it no longer matters in what direction we are going so long as we experience the unthinking exhilaration of movement? Such exhilaration does of course appeal more to youth than to others and it is surely significant that in the underdeveloped countries, some forty per cent of the population consists of people under the age of fifteen. Apart from their reproductive capacity over the next decade, youth is a period of excitement and dynamism rather than one of reflection and prudence, and it is doubtful if an appeal to them to postpone, voluntarily, immediate gratifications in the interests of themselves and their descendants would be successful. One thing, however, is certain and that is that

---

[14] I am well aware, as was Huxley, that in evolutionary terms man has exhibited a very rapid rate of biological growth, but we are speaking in terms of millions of years. 'Man of today, the atomic manipulator, the aeronaut who flies faster than sound, has precisely the same brain and body as his ancestors of 20,000 years ago who painted the last Ice-Age mammoths on the walls of caves in France.' Loren Eiseley, *The Immense Journey* (New York 1946), p. 89.

anyone who reads Toffler's book will realize we are, as yet, merely stepping over the threshold of change.

A permissible question, however, is what lies beyond that threshold – another room or simply an abyss? The dinosaur apparently became extinct because of its small brain. Man could easily repeat the process, not because of any mental deficiency but conversely and ironically because of his inability or unwillingness to curb, or at least redirect, his excessive brain-power, coupled with, and resulting in, his *infinite* materialistic expectations in a *finite* world – in brief, die from 'over-success'.

In the following chapters an attempt will be made to suggest ways in which education can help to eradicate or ameliorate some of the tensions and neuroses so evident in contemporary society. There are, of course, those who welcome tension and violence, or what has come to be described in some cosy educational circles as 'creative conflict'. Some who hold such views may be subconsciously motivated by the Freudian 'cult of unpleasure'; others see in the various 'liberation' movements which have mushroomed over the past two decades, hopeful signs of an emerging equal distribution of natural resources and a basis for a more just and equitable society. From these somewhat naïve Utopians I must dissent. Violence, as even a cursory study of history shows, has never resulted in a truly just or equitable society but on the contrary, as Orwell's *Animal Farm* reveals, merely provides an excuse for an emotional blow-out, followed inevitably by a repressive tyranny. It is clearly expressed in the following from J. Lasserre's article, '*Révolution et non-violence*' :[15]

> We do not believe that peace can come out of violence, that justice can issue from generalized criminality, that respect for man can emerge from contemptuousness. Hatred and crime result neither in justice nor in reconciliation, but in bitterness, cowardice, vice and crime . . . Ultimately, the cruellest and most clamorous . . . take over – the toughest, not the most just. And the revolution is aborted under the dictatorship of a new tyrant. How can you defend and build man when you begin by suppressing and destroying men?

If anyone questions the foregoing, the names of Cromwell,

---

[15] *Cahiers de la réconciliation* (Paris, 1967), pp. 34–36. Quoted in *Violence*, Jacques Ellul (London 1970).

Robespierre, Napoleon, Lenin, Stalin and Hitler should allow at least some consideration for Lasserre's thoughts.[16]

---

[16] The following from *The Crisis of Our Age* by the Harvard sociologist Pitirim Sorokin (who substantiates his statement statistically) is relevant:

'In the course of human history several thousand revolutions have been launched with a view to establishing a paradise on earth. And they are still proceeding at full blast, in spite of the fact that practically none of them has ever achieved its purpose . . . And we observe *"homo sapiens"* still engrossed in this crazy quest. From this standpoint, the history of human progress is indeed a history of incurable human stupidity!'

CHAPTER II

Change and Progress

———————◆———————

The pleasures of sudden wonder are soon exhausted
and the mind can only repose on the stability of
truth.
SAMUEL JOHNSON: *Preface to Shakespeare*

———————◆———————

In the light of what I have already written, I would like
to suggest that for some time past we may have been posing
the wrong questions and that instead of discussing how man
can adapt to technological advances, we should instead begin
to ask how much change is desirable, or indeed supportable in
terms of his emotional, physical, aesthetic and spiritual needs.
In other words is man made for technology, or is technology
made for man?

For too long, change has uncritically been regarded as
synonymous with progress, but first a few voices and now
many more are questioning the basic assumptions of such a
view. In a recent convocation address, President John Howard
of Rockford College, Illinois expressed himself as follows:

> The grand sweep towards an even brighter day has lost its
> momentum. . . . We have lots of things on the increase –
> hostilities and polarities, psychoses and neuroses, air and
> water impurities, an over-production of babies – but few
> people would claim that these abundancies or any others
> add up to progress.[1]

To those who would regard the above as the outpourings
of a bigoted obscurantist, I would simply suggest that if one
saw a blind man tottering precariously on the edge of a cliff,
one's instinctive reaction would be to counsel him to remain

———————————————————————————————————

[1] 'The Innovation Mirage', delivered on September 9, 1970.

immobile and then to take a step backwards. Western society, blinded by its technological sophistication and almost completely neglectful of the things of the spirit, resembles in many ways just such a situation. As a consequence we have produced a society consisting of technological giants and moral pygmies. Surely in these circumstances the term 'reactionary' should not be uncritically and unreservedly a term of abuse; and presumably thinking man does not want to rule out entirely the possibility that somewhere in the past society may have taken a wrong turning, and that it might be as well to examine without fear or prejudice the roots of our present malaise.

At the moment most people have comfortably turned their backs on 'eco-catastrophe', having decided that technology will in due course provide the answers to the problems which technology has created. This is about as sensible as to administer further doses of arsenic to one already suffering from arsenical poisoning. Those who hold such opinions resemble a motorist who, having encountered thick fog, decides to accelerate in order to get through it swiftly. The prudent driver would surely slow down or even *stop*.

It is, perhaps, interesting in the context of the foregoing, to examine the role of authors, artists and scientists in society prior to the nineteenth century, contrasted with their more recent attitudes. (I am fully aware of my temerity at this juncture, but can only hope that some readers will share with me Samuel Johnson's enthusiasm for the 'grandeur of generality'.)

It was Hegel, in the early nineteenth century, who coined the term 'alienation', leaving it to Marx to give the expression political significance. What is undeniably true is that with a few, very rare, exceptions most of the great English authors prior to 1800 were emphatically *not* alienated from society. Chaucer, while he was writing the *Canterbury Tales*, occupied a high position in what today would be called the civil service; Spenser, when he began *The Faerie Queen*, was secretary to the 'Governor' of Ireland; Sir Philip Sidney was both accomplished courtier and soldier; Bacon, Lord Chancellor of England. Shakespeare, having amassed a considerable fortune from his plays and from innumerable business deals, took out a coat-of-arms and retired to a comfortable and far from modest house in his native Stratford; Donne ended his career as Dean of St Paul's, and Milton held office in

Cromwell's Council of State and blinded himself on account of his devotion to the Puritan cause. John Dryden surrounded himself with literary cronies at Will's Coffee House where, it was maintained, 'a pinch out of his snuff-box' was equal to 'taking a degree in the academy of wit'; Swift, despite his apparent misanthropy (he left a considerable portion of his estate to the poor), was a career clergyman, Dean of St. Patrick's Cathedral, Dublin, and extremely active in both English and Irish political affairs. Richardson was a master-printer, Fielding an energetic and humane London magistrate, while both Pope and Johnson (although for different reasons) abhorred solitude and cultivated society assiduously.[2] There were, obviously, exceptions to the foregoing, but there does appear to have been a general pattern and these creative artists clearly did *not* experience a sense of alienation and *angst* to nearly the same degree as do those of a later period.

The watershed seems to have occurred approximately half-way through the eighteenth century and coincides, appropriately, with the career and writings of Jean-Jacques Rousseau, 'the man born without a skin', the archetypal, introspective outsider and alienated man. His life and works exhibit a mass of contradictions and paradoxes. Inspired by his friend, Diderot, he wrote a prize-winning discourse that denounced the arts and sciences as detrimental to the happiness of man, and yet was to make his living by his pen; his vaunted hatred and contempt for society concealed a deep-rooted paranoia and a desire for social acceptance. Professing to detest the aristocracy, he could obtain sexual satisfaction only from high-born women, and having abandoned his five illegitimate babies to the horrors of an eighteenth-century Parisian foundling-home, he proceeded to write a classical treatise on the rearing and education of children! Yet beneath all this was an ultra-sensitive being, a conscious artist endowed with prophetic vision. He, alone among his contemporaries, foresaw the long-range result of the 'Enlightenment' would be a tragic loss in terms of man's spiritual, aesthetic and social needs. A few decades later, Blake, confronting the brutalizing and de-humanizing effects of the beginnings of the industrial revolution, asked in rhetorical anguish :

---

[2] Their 'contentment' was not solely dependent on being comfortably off. Johnson recalls how when he and Richard Savage, lacking money to provide accommodation for the night, tramped the streets of London vowing 'they would stand by their country'.

And was Jerusalem builded here
Among these dark Satanic Mills?

I have chronicled in *Trousered Apes* the growing darkness of the artistic vision – Tennyson's spiritual struggle expressed in *In Memoriam,* yielding to the *fin-de-siècle* decadents and thence by stages to the contemporary hideous imaginings of Genet, Beckett and Pinter – a vision admirably described by the American critic George Wellwarth, in *The Theatre of Protest and Paradox,* as 'death-oriented hopelessness'. Perhaps in my earlier work I was too severe in my strictures on the literary and social significance of contemporary artists and, quite possibly, as I then suggested was inevitable, their vision has affected me. However, Ezra Pound has called artists 'the antennae of the human race' and Marshall McLuhan has defined art as 'a radar which acts as an early alarm system, enabling us to discover social and psychic targets in lots of time to prepare to cope with them.'

Both writers are implying that the creative artist, because of his greater sensitivity, is more aware than other men of the trends in his contemporary society which will shape the future. The artist is thus regarded as a prophet or seer. If one accepts this view, then what future is presaged by contemporary art, saturated as it is with violence and animalism and with the 'death-oriented hopelessness' to which Wellwarth refers? Can we recover any of that order, harmony and balance which characterized the poetry of Pope, the music of Mozart, the paintings of Watteau, the landscaping of William Kent, if our relationship with Nature and the environment is increasingly disordered, inharmonious and above all *unbalanced*?

Perhaps I am not sufficiently a creature of my own time to welcome stridency, divisiveness, militancy and disorder as presaging the dawn of an age which Shelley in *Prometheus Unbound* (1819) optimistically looked forward to – an age in which

> . . . man remains
> Sceptreless, free, uncircumscribed
> . . . equal, unclassed, tribeless and nationless
> Exempt from awe, worship, degree, the king
> Over himself.[3]

---

[3] Act III, lines 193–197.

Even were this to be the final outcome of revolutions, 'wars of liberation' and other 'advanced causes (of which I have already expressed doubt), the result would seem to resemble what geologists refer to as a peneplain – an almost totally flat, featureless landscape devoid of that essential *variety* without which human life and experiences would be unimaginably dull, and tolerable only to witless vegetables; a social version of international 'slab' architecture which is making London much more physically similar to New York than either is to, let us say, Burford, Oxfordshire or Charlottesville, Virginia.

Lord Clark concluded his remarkable television series, *Civilization*, with these words, which perhaps symbolize the ultimate goal of any educational or religious training worthy of the name :

> I believe that order is better than chaos, creation better than destruction. I prefer gentleness to violence, forgiveness to vendetta. On the whole I think that knowledge is preferable to ignorance, and I am sure that *human sympathy is more valuable than ideology* . . . I believe in courtesy, the ritual by which we avoid hurting other people's feelings by satisfying our own egos. And I think we should remember that *we are a part of a great whole,* which for convenience we call nature. All living things are our brothers and sisters. [My italics]

Matthew Arnold, in the nineteenth century, maintained that two powers must concur for an artistic masterpiece to come into existence, 'the power of the man and the power of the moment', and the man, he added, is not enough without the moment. The question which must occur to any sensitive observer of the contemporary scene is : Can *great* and *enduring* works of art (and this term includes literature, painting, sculpture, music and architecture) be produced by men and women living in a society for which the majority feels at best contempt and at worst a deep loathing and abhorrence? One obvious danger in the present situation lies in the fact that since so many talented artists do display marked anti-social tendencies, both public and critics may be fooled into mistaking mere anti-social posturing for genius. (There is, in fact, abundant evidence that this has already occurred.) A much greater danger, however, lies in the production and wide dissemination of books, plays and poems saturated with hatred and disgust, conveying only hopelessness and negation

B

to a culture, and indeed a species, already suffering a visible and palpable loss of nerve.

To those who would question the necessity for great and enduring art, I would reply as follows. It is that which over the centuries has *sustained* and *elevated* mankind; it represents a conquest by humanity over the diverse and bewildering complexities of human nature and of the surrounding world; it glories in both the natural and human scene. While recognizing that man can be (and frequently is) guilty of great cruelty and evil, it yet also depicts him as being *capable* of displaying heroic and self-sacrificing traits. It presents, in short, a balanced and total view of the struggle between the light and the dark forces inherent in human nature. At its best it consoles man by making him aware of the limitations of his *own* nature, while at the same time stressing the enduring qualities and courage of *human* nature.

If one examines the physical sciences, a somewhat similar pattern may be discerned in the gradual secularization of those who formerly styled themselves (and the title is revealing) natural philosophers.[4] In *Man and His Universe* Langdon-Davies writes as follows :

> The whole history of science has been a direct search for God, deliberate and conscious, until well into the eighteenth century. . . . Copernicus, Kepler, Galileo, Newton, Leibnitz and the rest did not merely believe in God in an orthodox sort of way; they believed that their work told humanity more about God than had been known before.[5]

This statement is to a great extent true, but one must remember that Plato's central doctrine that God was the measure of all things was quickly challenged by the doctrine of Protagoras that *man* was the measure of all things. Moreover, Democritus, who can be described as the father of modern scepticism and empiricism, saw the world as consisting simply of atoms and a void. Today, thinking men are still

---

[4] The term 'scientist' was coined by William Whewell as recently as 1840.

[5] Nearer our own time Einstein, when asked by a Professor of Philosophy at the University of California how the theory of relativity had been arrived at, replied that he had discovered it because he was so 'firmly convinced of the harmony of the universe'. Moreover despite some of the implications of his early work he resolutely opposed the idea that 'God plays dice with the world.' (See Ronald W. Clark's *Einstein: The Life and Times*. London, 1973.)

split largely into two camps; the one asserting that man is merely a walking bag of sea-water or a complex but predictable collection of reactions to various stimuli; the other maintaining that this is a case of crass temporal provincialism and that science and the scientific method pose at least as many questions as they answer and that both modern science and poetry end in a metaphor.[6] It may be recalled that A. R. Wallace, Darwin's contemporary and co-discoverer with him of the principles of natural selection, challenged the Darwinian attitude to man when he asserted that artistic, musical and mechanical abilities could not be explained solely through a theory dependent on a struggle for existence. Some unknown spiritual element, Wallace insisted, must have contributed to the evolution of the human mind.

The zoologist, Sir Alister Hardy, F.R.S., indicated in his Gifford lectures that mankind always appears to be enslaved by some fashionable dogma. In the middle ages men suffered from 'an appalling mental nightmare' – the belief in a personal devil in a real and *localized* Hell, not symbolically but quite literally. Hardy suggests that although it may horrify some of his colleagues, Bernard Shaw's gibe that science has become the superstition of the twentieth century yet may deserve to be taken seriously :

> It is not, of course, science itself that constitutes the superstition, but the dogmatism that many of its exponents have added to it. I passionately believe in the validity of science and the scientific method, but just as strongly do I deplore the false assertions that *science* finds the mystery of the mind-body relationship to be unreal and has classed consciousness as an irrelevant illusion. Such dogmatic materialism could lead in the future to a world even more horrific than that created by the mediaeval mind, a future such as Aldous Huxley warned us of; or it could lead to our complete destruction, a possibility that was not even on the horizon when he wrote *Brave New World*.[7]

---

[6] 'Science is dumb if we ask it to explain the greatest human works or emotions or experiences. . . . Here we are in a mysterious, yet familiar world which belongs to religion, poetry and arts but not to Science. Yet these things as well as atoms and elements and cells, are part of the world.' Sir Richard Livingstone, *Some Tasks for Education*, pp. 8, 9.

[7] *The Divine Flame: Natural History and Religion* (London 1966), pp. 18, 19.

The 'complete destruction' to which Hardy refers in the foregoing is presumably that by thermo-nuclear warfare, but there is another more insidious threat to the human race and that is the threat to the soul of man. As C. S. Lewis once pointed out, when one sees *through* everything, one sees in effect *nothing*. This is the nihilism which is the social and cultural product of scientific scepticism and has led, step by step to historical determinism, in which man feels himself increasingly a spectator of the contemporary scene, powerless to affect its gadarene march in any significant way.

One other point deserves mention here and that is that technology is slowly but surely eroding the entire political system. In 1972, the population of the United States solemnly proceeded to the polls and duly elected their President to a further period of incumbency of the White House, not realizing that the real forces which shape and will shape their lives – the brain biologists, the IBM specialists, the atomic physicists, the controllers and producers of the mass-media and a host of assorted technocrats – are not subject to the restraints of the democratic process. (Whatever the outcome of the Watergate enquiry, one thing is certain, and that is that 'Trial by Television' has now become a fact of American political life.) These are the true wielders of power ('power' in this context meaning the ability to determine what happens to the physical and mental life of the populace at large), and all the men in the White House or Downing Street or, possibly, even in the Kremlin can do is demonstrate their dwindling ability to exercise any real control over the pace or desirability of change.[8] We do not vote for more progress or less, swifter change or slower. If we *could* elect the President of IBM or the Atomic Energy Commission there might still be some point to it all. But we do not, and power is passed from the electorate to the technocrats who are not the scientists but merely those who use the discoveries of modern science, often in an unthinking and irresponsible fashion. In the following chapter some further aspects of the cause of the technological revolution, and the implications thereof, will be discussed.

---

[8] For a full analysis of this question see Jacques Ellul's *The Political Illusion* (New York, 1967).

CHAPTER III

Knowledge and Wisdom

Yet I doubt not thro' the ages one increasing purpose
runs,
And the thoughts of men are widen'd with the process
of the suns . . .
Knowledge comes but wisdom lingers, and I linger on
the shore,
And the individual withers, and the world is more
and more.

TENNYSON : *Locksley Hall* (1842)

The 'knowledge explosion' (to which I referred in Chapter I),
at once amplified and symbolized by the paper-back revolution,
xeroxing and other photographic reproduction methods, is
obviously technological in origin, and in certain scientific
fields knowledge is doubling every five years. Although the
results are generally unthinkingly applauded (the dissemination of knowledge being, in our post-lapsarian state, regarded
as the *summum bonum*), yet even here a question or two is,
perhaps, permissible.

Firstly, are we quite certain that *everyone* is mentally and
morally prepared for the deluge of information which pours
from the world's presses? One does not need to be a particularly perceptive critic to realize that, as I have suggested,
there is a pervasive death-wish inherent in much of contemporary literature and philosophy, thinly disguised under
fashionable forms of nihilism and 'protests against the
cosmos'. Have we yet fully taken into account the social and
cultural effects of the paper-back revolution? For it coincides
with new concepts expounded by, and intended for, tough,
well-balanced adult minds and only too often brings to an
ever-increasing youthful audience a distorted message –
instant gratification of all appetites with no subsequent bill to

pay – a doctrine directly hostile to the very basis of human survival and, if unchecked, destined to produce eco-catastrophe. (When payment is, inevitably, exacted, a feeling of mingled despair and cynicism appears to be the result). Furthermore, as an article in the September 1972 issue of the *British Medical Journal* observes, 'for many people immaturity extends far beyond childhood into adult life – into middle age and beyond. Civilized society accepts the obligation of protecting its children from influences harmful to their health.

To impose reasonable safeguards for the benefit of immature adults is a far more difficult matter unless they are seriously defective. But when relatively healthy people decry attempts to limit the citizen's freedom of expression they should remember that limits already exist and that the weaker members of a community deserve protection, not exploitation.'

I do not, of course, mean to imply that those who formulate such ultimately reductionist concepts intend this particular result; it is merely the outcome of an egalitarian society in which everything must be made available to all immediately. Let me cite an example. Some years ago I attended a showing of the film *Bridge on the River Kwai* at a cinema in a 'poor' section of a British city. In the film Alec Guinness, playing an army colonel, is punished by his Japanese captors for refusing to co-operate fully in the building of a bridge over a remote river. He is incarcerated for several days in a small tin shed, exposed to the scorching sun, unable to stretch his limbs adequately. Finally, on release, he staggers out, his legs barely able to support him after his cramped ordeal. The makers of the film obviously wished to communicate the colonel's heroism and dignity in humiliating circumstances, but the particular audience in whose company I watched the film, rocked with laughter at Guinness's pathetic attempt to walk upright and treated the spectacle as they would have done a Chaplin comedy. (I subsequently had to see the film again with a more responsible audience, to rid myself of the nausea I experienced at the first viewing.)

It might be salutary for Stanley Kubrick and other avant-garde film-makers to view their productions, not in a cosy private studio, surrounded by intellectuals who 'understand' the message, but in an ordinary cinema where the audience just *might* react to *Clockwork Orange*, for example, in as bizarre and unpredictable a fashion as the audience which I have just described.

The question is not so simple as it was in the comparatively élitist society of John Stuart Mill's time. It is no longer a straightforward either/or between a discontented Socrates and a contented pig; one must now seriously raise the possibility that the net, social result of the knowledge explosion may be a society consisting largely of semi-educated, psychologically disturbed human beings. The high incidence of mental illness, the growing dependence on various drugs would seem to indicate that growing numbers have lost, or are losing, what Teilhard de Chardin called 'that essential taste for life'.[1]

Secondly (and here I feel a greater prospect of general agreement) if these words are published, then trees, or at least part of a tree, will have to be sacrificed in order to provide the necessary paper. The ecological equation is all to obvious, but few appear to have faced up to its full implications. Newspapers, magazines, journals, hard- and paper-backed books, and articles on a variety of subjects, some serious but the majority dealing with trivia, flood the bookstores and news-stands. What Samuel Johnson in the eighteenth century acidly referred to as 'that monstrous conspiracy for the destruction of paper', has increased in volume until it threatens to overwhelm us, not only mentally but also physically. Taylor in *Rethink*[2] draws an interesting comparison between man being reduced to physical insignificance by the skyscraper and to mental insignificance by 'the richness of the culture, by the flood of data too great to absorb'. In this respect, perhaps the American university imperative for promotion should be amended to 'Publish *and* Perish'.)

Again it is largely a question of numbers and economics. In Johnson's day, a comparatively small number of writers catered to the tastes and desires of a fairly small, homogeneous, literate minority.[3] It is perhaps worth noting that through the mass media we are constantly being barraged

---

[1] In *Rethink*, G. R. Taylor suggests that about 1,500 people attempt suicide *every day* in the U.S. alone.

[2] London, 1972.

[3] Ian Watt in *The Rise of the Novel* (London, 1954) calculates the British reading public in the 1790s as comprising some 80,000 out of a population of six million, and adds that only one person in a hundred bought a weekly newspaper.

with vivid presentations of events, often in remote parts of the world, over which we obviously can exert no control. A century or more ago our great-grandparents were generally faced with a much more localized situation over which, either by vote or other methods of pressure, they were able to feel they had some control. Our knowledge of affairs is a hundred times wider than theirs, and yet we are still endowed with precisely the same power – that is to say, one vote – and the consequent feeling of helplessness may well be an additional component in the rising rate of general frustration.

Today, more and more writers are catering to a far greater public with infinitely more varied and specialized tastes than ever before. This is not in any way to imply censorship but one may question if a publisher has an inalienable right to squander dwindling and essential natural resources merely to enrich himself and his clients. (Publishers might perhaps re-tort that I am personally compounding the offence and also that compared with the avalanche of government forms they are comparatively guiltless.)

Thirdly, I would like to concur with the remarks of Taylor, quoted previously, and suggest that we have already too much factual information for our culture to absorb, and in conse-quence we are packing this knowledge into computers in the somewhat desperate hope that they will solve our problems for us. Computers are certainly impressive objects; they can store millions of facts effortlessly in their 'brains', but they do not *understand* and above all, they do not *feel* (in human terms) one of the facts which they hoard. The results are everywhere in evidence – a widespread feeling of alienation and helplessness in the presence of faceless, often contradictory, mechanically-dispensed instructions, information and advice. After all, a world dominated by statistics is a poor substitute for one of true human understanding, and of the compassion which comes from such understanding.

The 'Pill' and the Bomb, superficially, have made chastity and patriotism questionable virtues. The stigma, and indeed the probability of an unwanted child having been more or less removed, the young and also the not-so-young now confidently and logically assert that the old sexual morality was founded on nothing more virtuous than fear, and since the foundation has gone the entire edifice must tumble. The Bomb has rendered national rivalries obsolete or at least obsolescent, and made the thoughtful of all ages tend more and more to a position of pacificism. All the sacred concepts of previous generations, together with their outward symbols, are being questioned and, for the most part, rejected.[4] If the mass media have created what Marshall McLuhan has called 'the global village', then the Bomb has led to a state of mind best expressed by Auden : 'We must love one another or die.' Unfortunately, although the intelligentsia in most countries of the world acknowledge the necessity for a re-pudiation of militarism and outmoded jingoism, the vast majority of the masses still cling to the old, nationalistic (and perhaps even more natural) emotions, often fanned and encouraged by powerful (if myopic) vested interests. I would be willing to assert that for every person who would intellectu-ally assent to Auden's statement, there are hundreds, possibly thousands (in both the Orient and Occident) who would sooner proudly, if unthinkingly, proclaim : 'My country, right or wrong.'

Meanwhile, at universities throughout the world, the most physically healthy generation of youth ever bred finds its energy and courage disappearing in the dehumanized world of 'plastics'. Regarding themselves (and quite rightly) as simply material for computers (an inevitable result of the co-existence of such machines with eight million students in the United States alone),[5] they react, predictably and often violently, to the bursting 'academic container'. Significantly, it is at those universities with enrolments in tens of thousands that the more serious outbreaks have occurred. These, in cer-tain instances, have reached such intense proportions that one may wonder if youth, baulked of the traditional initiation of

---

[4] The following from Malcolm Muggeridge's *Chronicles of Wasted Time* (London, 1972, p. 15) is perhaps symptomatic of a widespread feeling :
'By the same token, a strange certainty has possessed me, almost since I can remember, that the Lord Mayor riding in his coach, the Lord Chancellor seated on his Woolsack, Honourable and Right Honourable Members facing one another across the floor of the House of Commons, were somehow the end of a line. That soon there would be no more Lord Mayors, Lord Chancellors, Honourable and Right Honourable Members, the Mother of Parliaments having reached her time of life or menopause, and become incapable of any further pro-creation.'

[5] Well in excess of 20,000 computers are being installed in the United States every year and even in the United Kingdom the figure is approximately 1,000.

B*

old-fashioned warfare, is not determined to have its baptism
of fire, even while vociferously repudiating any conventional
call to arms.[6]

The foregoing are just some of the effects of the technological revolution, but the truly ominous aspects lie in the
field of the biological sciences. I shall deal here with only
two disturbing and recent experiments, allowing them to
exemplify a trend. In 1963, at Cornell University, Professor
F. C. Steward 'cloned' a carrot; that is to say he took cells from
a single carrot and by a chemical process which need not be
elaborated here, was able to produce nearly 100,000 *identical*
carrots and theoretically an *infinite* number, Taylor, writing
in *The Biological Time Bomb* in 1968, suggested that the
$64,000 dollar question was, of course, whether or not the
same process could be effective with animal cells. Within
weeks of my reading Taylor's book it had been done, with a
frog, at Oxford. Such is the speed of technological communication in the 'hot-house' of the global village. Referring
to cloning, Alvin Toffler in *Future Shock* makes the following observations, assuming quite logically that if the process can be applied to frogs it can also be applied to human
beings :

> There is a certain charm to the idea of Albert Einstein
> bequeathing copies of himself to posterity. But what of
> Adolf Hitler? Should there be laws to regulate cloning?

Do we in fact want a whole race of Mozarts or of Ghengis
Khans, super athletes or super-intellectuals – and which
among us is *to make the choice*?

Again, recently a brain was removed from a dog and kept
artificially alive by means of blood being pumped through it
from successive batteries of involuntary 'serf' dogs. Theoretically, at least, this bestows the power of granting at least a
measure of 'immortality' to the fortunate (or unfortunate)
creature selected for the experiment (provided blood-donors
are available), but the moral and ethical questions underlying
all this are overwhelming. Who shall live? On what grounds
do we select – artistically, physically, militaristically, athletic-

---

[6] 'Many believe that some young people join in virulent protests because they *enjoy* the clashes with authority. It may be no coincidence
that the current rise in civilian violence roughly corresponds with the
time that a third world war might have been expected.' Dr. H. J.
Campbell, *The Pleasure Areas* (London 1973).

ally?[7] People in the comparatively near future may well be able to marry a semi-artificial partner, to choose their children's sex, to eradicate their own memories and assume vicarious ones. Taylor even suggests that one day one may be introduced to a single person with the explanation 'I should like you to meet my uncle and nephew. They were killed in an auto crash but salvaged in parts.' Referring to these and other mind-boggling 'advances' Taylor proceeds to express himself as follows:

> Having surveyed the work of biologists in many countries, having listened to their own comments on the implications of such work, to me, at least, it is clear that the social and personal costs of adapting to this new knowledge will be terrifyingly, unacceptably high unless we make a major, conscious effort to regulate the pace and scope of development, instead of letting it control us. There is still time to stop. Soon it will be too late, even if we wish to.[8]

The question inherent in all the foregoing is quite simply : Can man advance on his present course without sacrificing what we have hitherto regarded as 'human' nature? For the first time we are able, not merely to appreciate intellectually a theory of evolution, but actually to modify and change the direction of such evolution in more or less any way we please. Incidentally, it is just beginning to be realized that the

---

[7] I cannot resist quoting the following from the third book of *Gulliver's Travels* ('A Voyage to Laputa, Balnibarbi, Glubbdubdrib, Luggnagg and Japan') in which Swift describes the immortal 'Struldbruggs':

'When they come to fourscore years, which is reckoned the extremity of living in this country, they had not only all the follies and infirmities of other old men, but many more which arose from the dreadful prospect of never dying. They were not only opinionate, peevish, covetous, morose, vain, talkative, but incapable of friendship and dead to all natural affection, which never descended below their grandchildren. Envy and impotent desires are their prevailing passions. . . . They have no remembrance of anything but what they learnt and observed in their youth and middle age and even that is very imperfect. And for the truth or particulars of any fact, it is safer to depend on common traditions than upon their best recollections. The least miserable among them appear to be those who turn to dotage, and entirely lose their memories; these meet with more pity and assistance because they want many bad qualities which abound in others.'

[8] *The Biological Time Bomb* (New York, 1968) p. 24.

intellectual sophistication necessary to formulate an evolutionary theory was itself part of the evolutionary process. Similarly
the *choice* to direct it is perhaps a sign of supra-sophistica-
tion. The *method* already exists and nothing that man *can*
do has through recorded history remained undone, no matter
how harmful or indeed catastrophic the outcome.

When the team under Rutherford split the atom at Cambridge it was a superb example of sophisticated scientific
ability, and as a piece of *pure* science must attract admiration. Only one unacquainted with the horrors of Nagasaki
and Hiroshima could claim, however, that mankind was
ethically or morally equipped to handle the inevitable extension and application of Rutherford's work.

If this was true of the atom bomb, how much more so is it
of the myriad discoveries which have taken place in the
physical sciences, particularly biology, over the past twenty
years. Even Alvin Toffler, one of the more optimistic of
'*futurists*', concedes that the 'nature of what can and will be
done exceeds anything that man is, as yet, psychologically or
morally prepared to live with.'

The question then arises : what do we, collectively and
individually, do about it? It is obviously too important to be
left to the specialists for as Marshall McLuhan has observed
a specialist is 'one who never makes small mistakes while
moving towards the grand fallacy.'

At the same time one must beware of over-reaction to these
problems and attempt to move cautiously between those
who have espoused abstract thought, divorced from any
passion, and those who rely totally on passion and reject
thought. As I have suggested elsewhere, no literary work
has been so consistently and persistently misunderstood as
the fourth book of *Gulliver's Travels*. Gulliver, as readers
may recall, was faced with the apparent choice of emulating
the Houyhnhnms, symbols of abstract, dehumanized reason,
or degenerating into the bestial state epitomized by the
Yahoos. Both alternatives were equally repugnant to one
such as Swift — a product of the classical, humanist tradition — and Gulliver, swooning at the smell of his wife and
children upon his return home, infatuated with the horses and
neighing instead of speaking, is mercilessly satirized for his
failure to espouse the *via media* and continue to be a Man.

The views expressed by C. P. Snow and F. R. Leavis in the
almost-forgotten debate on the 'Two Cultures' in the early

sixties represent graphically the dichotomy of thought which persists even today. The former's assertion that scientists have 'the future in their bones', must, however, strike even the most blinkered devotee of science as a somewhat ambiguous accolade (and Snow himself has considerably modified his earlier view), while Leavis's rejoinder, although saturated with humanist ideals and an attack on blatant materialism, was scarcely humane in its treatment of Snow's reputation as a novelist or indeed as a man. One must attempt to avoid such polarities and be particularly suspicious of the bland inducements of the behaviourist school as epitomized by B. F. Skinner and others. In his latest book *Beyond Freedom and Dignity*,[9] Skinner recognizes fully the 'terrifying problems that face us in the world today' and indeed quotes C. D. Darlington to good effect:

> Every new source from which man has increased his power on the earth has been used to diminish the prospects of his successors. All his progress has been made at the expense of damage to his environment which he cannot repair and could not foresee.

Skinner then proceeds to outline *his* solution to all our contemporary ills. His basic thesis is that the concepts of human dignity and freedom belong to a pre-scientific age. In the scientific view, he maintains, a person's behaviour and character are shaped by genetic endowments, traceable ultimately to the evolutionary history of the human species and by the environmental circumstances to which, as an individual, he or she has been exposed. If one adopts this viewpoint then obviously praise and blame, reward and punishment are outmoded, as is the whole question of free-will and choice, and one is left with a curious type of Calvinism, though divorced from the fear of hell-fire. 'Autonomous' (that is to say individual) man is also a myth created by what Skinner terms the 'literatures of freedom and dignity', which he suggests were once brilliant and necessary exercices in opposing the forces of tyranny but which he believes are no longer appropriate to the task.

This somewhat bleak view of human nature does not fill Dr. Skinner with gloom, however. His position can be summed up in the words of T. H. Huxley:

---

[9] London 1972.

If some great power would agree to make me always think what is true and do what is right, on condition of being some sort of clock, wound up every morning before I get out of bed, I should close instantly with the offer.

Skinner's solutions to the problems of the modern world are (given his thesis) predictable. Utopia can be achieved if we all submit to being conditioned, and if we allow our energies to be directed towards changing the physical and social environment in which we live and which in turn shapes us. What he calls for is a 'technology of behaviour', and this raises yet another problem. Can we rely on the benevolence of cultural technologists or would they simply create a new world in their own image, and produce a new form of tyranny even more constraining and enduring than any previously imagined because their conditioned 'captives' will not only be bereft of a means of escape but also devoid even of the imagination to realize that they are, in fact, captives?[10]

In discussing his future Utopian state, Skinner does recognize that it will not be liked by people 'as they are now but it will be liked by those who live in it. . . . A world that would be "liked" by contemporary people would perpetuate the *status quo* and that *status quo* is an anxiety-ridden world facing the seemingly insurmountable problems of over-population, the depletion and eventual exhaustion of natural resources, the pollution of the environment and the possibility of a nuclear holocaust.'

The latter part of the foregoing is unfortunately true, and a truth does not cease to be true simply because it is un-palatable. Skinner's solution, however − Peoples of the world unite; you have nothing to lose but the illusion of your indi-vidual selves − is almost as repugnant, and after reading his

---

[10] Even as I write these words, a remarkable example of 'conditioning', not of humans but of dolphins and whales, is revealed in an article in the *International Herald-Tribune* (20 February, 1973):

'James Fitzgerald, identified as a pioneer in dolphin research for the intelligence community and the Navy told CBS that researchers have been able to programme dolphins "and keep them under control for distances of up to several miles. . . . You can use acoustics homing, acoustics beam-riding. You can use a radio link or you can have an inertial device in the gadget that they're towing which can tell them to go right or left or they're on course." According to CBS the Navy's dolphins have been trained to attack enemy divers, to ward off sharks, to place explosives and to monitor devices on ships.'

solution many will undoubtedly feel, with Dostoevsky, that even if it could be proved that human behaviour is totally determined 'man would still do something out of sheer perversity – he would create destruction and chaos just to gain his point . . . And if all this could in turn be analyzed and prevented by predicting that it would occur, then man would deliberately go mad to prove his point.'

St. Ignatius Loyola suggested that the ultimate sacrifice that God demanded of men was 'the sacrifice of the intellect'. It is ironic that Skinner, who is in a strange fashion the quintessence of twentieth-century intellect, should demand an infinitely greater sacrifice – the sacrifice of selfhood or of soul.[11] Nor, of course, is he alone in his views. Arthur Koestler, in *The Ghost in the Machine,* after pointing out, quite rightly, that man's intelligence has enabled him to build a hydrogen bomb but that this same intelligence has not produced a correspondingly high ethical code prohibiting him from using such a weapon, suggests that the *thinking* part of the human brain has never been able to control the passionate or *feeling* part, and on this account man remains emotionally in the Stone Age, while inhabiting the atomic era. Koestler's solution – some sort of 'brain-pill' (which could possibly be inserted through the water supplies or in some other way achieve universal application) to allow the rational faculty to exert constant control over the emotional – seems as unpalatable as Skinner's, and one is still left with the question : who or what agency would administer it? That *some* solution is needed, however, no one who has read thus far can seriously doubt.

---

[11] I would refer readers to Alister Hardy's remarks on this subject in Chapter II.

CHAPTER IV

Supra-culture and Anarchy

———◆———

And we are here as on a darkling plain
Swept with confused alarms of struggle and flight,
Where ignorant armies clash by night.
MATTHEW ARNOLD: *Dover Beach* (1867)

———◆———

Although undoubtedly many of our ills can be attributed to our post-lapsarian condition and to the perennial folly inherent in human nature, yet at the same time it seems that unless one subscribes to a totally deterministic view of man and engages in endless wrangles over the proportionate rôles of heredity and environment involved in the shaping of human character, then educational theory and practice must bear some of the responsibility for the sort of world we are living in and creating for our children. With the growing secularization of our schools, teacher-training colleges and universities, 'cleverness', as opposed to character, has tended to become the sole aim and criterion among many teachers and pupils. Coincidental with this has appeared an almost total rejection of Thomas Arnold's concept of a school as a social as well as an educational moulder.

Such an attitude it is felt, rightly or wrongly, smacks of paternalism, imperialism and other outmoded concepts, and militates against the *natural* development of the pupil. The history of the twentieth century, however, provides far too many examples of hideous atrocities (including well-meaning ones) committed by highly intelligent 'devils' for the prevalent attitude to be uncritically or complacently accepted. Jon Wynne-Tyson in his provocative book *The Civilised Alternative*[1]

---

[1] Fontwell, 1972, p. 190.

suggests that what 'we have not sufficiently woken up to as yet is that while doing away with the ritual and dogma of organized religion, we also deprived ourselves of the essential discipline – and consequently comfort – of those moral guidelines that have lain hidden like veins and arteries in the all too fleshly body of the established church.'

Perhaps a parallel could be drawn between the Arnoldean educational ideal and that of the church. Both stemmed from a classical tradition, with Christian overtones, and were based on the widely-held assumption that there was a corpus of truth, both religious and educational, which it was the duty of the clergy and schoolmasters to pass on to successive generations. Basically, such an attitude derived from Aristotle, who maintained that the aim of education was to make the pupil like and dislike what he *ought*. Mentors (both religious and secular) were thought to know more than their congregations or pupils and therefore to be in a position of authority; in certain instances this produced tyrannical figures and unjust situations but, as I recall from my own experiences some thirty years ago, the vast majority of teachers were decent, humane men and women and far from resenting their 'paternalistic' attitude most of us leaned heavily on them for advice and personal assistance, as well as deriving knowledge from their instruction.

It was what Taylor would have described as a 'patristic' society and had obvious limitations and defects. If, however, one examines the various components of the systems outlined below it can easily be seen that western society has swung from one extreme to the other in a matter of only decades.[2] The present educational view is evidently weighted towards

---

[2] The table below, taken from G. R. Taylor's *Rethink,* indicates with great clarity the polarities in question:

Patrism	*Matrism*
Restrictive, especially sex	Permissive, especially sex
Authoritarian	Democratic
Hierarchic	Egalitarian
Women: low status	Women: High status
Conservative	Adaptable
Looks to past	Looks to present or future
Pessimistic, depressive	Optimistic, euphoric
Self-control valued	Spontaneity valued
Homosexuality taboo	Incest taboo
Sexual jealousy	Lack of jealousy
Sky-father religion	Earth-mother or pantheist religion

egalitarianism, the underlying supposition being that since there is no generally agreed corpus of truth to be handed down, therefore both teacher and taught occupy roughly equal positions and can presumably happily pool their ignorance.

A short time ago, on a BBC television programme devoted to a discussion on the rôle of the teacher in contemporary society, a prominent British educator declared that the aim of the teacher should be 'to sow doubts in the minds of his pupils'. This is good, current orthodoxy and is simply a précis of Jules Henry, whom R. D. Laing quotes as follows in *The Divided Self*:

> If all through school the young are provoked to question the Ten Commandments, the sanctity of revealed religion, the foundations of patriotism, the profit-motive, the two-party system, monogamy, the laws of incest and so on,

there would be, says Laing, such a burst of creativity that 'society *would not know where to turn*' [my italics].

These views are, of course, simply extensions of scientific empiricism and philosophic scepticism to the field of education, but is there not a danger that the net result of such *total* questioning and probing may educationally result in a further reductionism, in young people 'seeing *through* everything' and ultimately 'seeing nothing?'[3] G. K. Chesterton once suggested that 'the only reason for having an open mind is the same as having an open mouth; so that eventually one can bite on something.' Hypercriticism can be as dangerous as a totally uncritical attitude, particularly if such hypercriticism is exclusively and facilely directed to perceiving the imperfections of all human institutions – government, church, colleges, laws, other people – to the absolute neglect of turning this same penetrating lens inward upon the self and developing a counter-balancing humility about one's *own* manifest frailties and imperfections.

---

[3] 'If you do not want to be sorry for your pupils when they have reached the age of thirty, you must be very careful how you introduce them to philosophical discussions. You must have seen how the young, when they get their first taste of it, treat argument as a form of sport solely for the purpose of contradiction. When someone has proved them wrong, they copy his methods to confute others, delighting like puppies in tugging and tearing at anyone who comes near them. And so after a long course of proving others wrong and being proved wrong themselves, they rush to the conclusion that all they once believed in is false.' Plato, *The Republic*.

It is in this respect that Rousseau and all his subsequent disciples have erred. He, and they, have naïvely assumed human nature to be good, not merely neutral. If men and women are bad then Society has corrupted their natural propensities and consequently, were all existing institutions to be destroyed, mankind could start all over again but *this* time create a better world. The flaw in the argument is, of course, that 'Society' is not some external system, super-imposed on a protesting humanity by a malevolent deity, but a natural outgrowth of individual and collective hopes, ambitions, passions, restraints, successes and errors.

Returning to Laing's suggestion, however, perhaps one may be allowed to indulge in one or two heterodox reactions. Firstly, is it not possible that we have already too much unanchored 'creativity' – a creativity based to a degree on a self-sufficient and undisciplined arrogance and not on pain-fully-acquired wisdom? The latter is almost always accom-panied by a sense of humility because no philosophical system that the mind of man can devise has yet been able to with-stand another man's ability to confute.[4]

An iconoclastic cleverness emanating from an unanchored intellect was the very quality with which Milton, himself a disillusioned revolutionary, endowed Satan – the symbol of ultimately purposeless energy and rebellion.[5] Such total oppo-sition to what is right, Milton suggests, springs from a pseudo-intellectual *pride*. None of the romantics who glorify in the 'free' spirit appear to have noticed, in their canonization of Satan as the hero of *Paradise Lost,* that both he and his 'angels' from the moment they decided to wage implacable war against God, or the natural law, became in fact merely *enslaved* puppets:

> To do ought good never will be our task,
> But ever to do ill our sole delight,
> *As being the contrary* to his high will
> Whom we resist.
> (*Paradise Lost,* I, 159–162, my italics)

---

[4] I am particularly fond of the following from Bernard Mandeville's *The Fable of the Bees* (1714): 'For we are ever pushing our reason which way soever we feel passion to draw it, and self-love pleads to all human creatures for their different views, still furnishing every individual with arguments to justify their inclinations.'
[5] Abbie Hoffman's *Revolution For The Hell Of It* is a good con-temporary example of such satanic traits.

Presumably, had God through an unthinkable whim become evil, Satan in his role of persistent and professional opposer would have had to perform a complete *volte-face* and once again exhibit (no doubt to the astonishment of Belial, Moloch, Beelzebub and his other consorts) diametrically opposed qualities, and become preternaturally virtuous.

It may also be recalled in this connection that after Satan's plan to revenge himself by suborning the *weakest* links in God's creation, Man, some of the fallen angels retired to a hill and there indulged in what C. S. Lewis once referred to as 'intellectual masturbation' – great fun but hardly productive in any sense :

> Others apart sat on a hill retir'd,
> In thoughts more elevate, and reason'd high
> Of providence, foreknowledge, will, and fate,
> Fix'd fate, free will, foreknowledge absolute,
> And found no end, in wand'ring mazes lost.
>
> (*Ibid.*, II, 557–561).

This Milton later described as 'vain wisdom all and false philosophy'.

Secondly, a plausible argument can be advanced, advocating an alternative to what Laing suggests; specifically that it is the duty of a teacher, whatever his personal ideology and views, ostensibly to *oppose* the ideas and beliefs of his pupils, thereby providing them with a necessary sounding-board on which the strengths and weaknesses of their arguments may be tested – winning either acceptance or rejection in the light of the teacher's greater knowledge and experience of life. It must be agonizing for so many of today's youthful radicals, particularly those at colleges and universities, to storm the citadel of entrenched adulthood with their intellectual battering-ram only to find that their mentors have sympathetically but frustratingly lowered the drawbridge, opened the gates and in certain extreme instances razed the very building to the ground, allowing the besiegers to career onwards with no challenge or hope of rebuttal.

Moreover, in the absence of any opposition, intellectual pride and arrogance may be fanned and enlarged to unhealthy extremes and a form of mental narcissism ensue.

Men have throughout history exhibited pride, which would appear to be a constant in human nature. In the eighteenth century, for example, the ownership of land and of a good pedigree were thought to be legitimate sources of pride; in the nineteenth century wealth supplanted them and today, with the virtual disappearance of a landed aristocracy and a tendency for the rich to be less ostentatious (one might almost say, furtive) about their wealth, an aristocracy of the intellect is replacing them – far less certain in that it is based on ideas rather than on things, and therefore more intolerant of those who question its basic suppositions and attitudes.

Surely, however, any education worthy of the name should convey, as a primary fact, that intellect is an hereditary gift, and is therefore no more a cause for pride or arrogance than the possession of land or wealth was in previous centuries. It is surely the *direction* in which the intellect is used which is of primary concern. Ownership of land did for the most part go hand-in-hand with a tangible sense of responsibility for its stewardship and cultivation; ownership of intellect need not, *of necessity,* recognize any such responsibility and can indeed exhibit on occasions an arrogant disdain for even elementary common-sense. There is, too, what Sir Richard Livingstone calls 'intellectual sadism', Goethe's 'spirit of eternal negation'. Livingstone describes it as 'believing itself to be a dislike of shams, sentimentality and affectation, a *ruthless* determination to reach truth. Its first reaction to any claim to greatness is suspicion. It looks behind the surface for mean motives and hidden corruptions, it watches for the crumbling of idols and the skeleton in the cupboard.'[6] Such a negative cynicism can only precipitate the crisis and drive yet another nail into the coffin of human hope and human dignity.

In its theoretical form it is manifest in an existential vacuum, a void and a feeling of emptiness; practically it spawns such destructive cults as the Theatre of the Absurd, together with a totally cynical attitude to duties coupled with an almost religious scrupulousness towards 'rights' (although why the latter should exist in an 'absurd' and meaningless universe is curiously overlooked). Such cynicism appears to reserve its accolades for men and women who transcend 'conventional' morality, however destructive of self and society such 'free' spirits may be. This 'freedom' is directly contrary to the *collective* survival of the species, since in an

---

[6] *Some Tasks for Education,* p. 77.

increasingly crowded society any further extension of one's own rights tends invariably and inexorably to infringe upon another's. In his *History of Western Philosophy,* Bertrand Russell makes the following observations on supra-egotism and its eventual effect upon society :

> Christianity has succeeded, to some extent, in taming the Ego, but economic, political, and intellectual causes stimulated revolt against the Churches, and the romantic movement brought the revolt into the sphere of morals. By encouraging a new lawless Ego it made social co-operation impossible, and left its disciples faced with the alternative of anarchy or despotism. Egoism, at first, made men expect from others a parental tenderness; but when they discovered with indignation that others had their own Ego, the disappointed desire for tenderness turned to hatred and violence. Man is not a solitary animal and as long as social life survives, self-realization cannot be the supreme principle of ethics.[7]

A few years ago, a poem composed by a student, of whose identity I am ignorant but who was at the time of its composition at the University of Berkeley, California, came into my possession. I shall quote it in full for it exhibits many characteristics of the life-style of the emerging, so-called 'alternative society', which makes that alternative at least as repugnant as the society it rejects :

For My Son

I long to run freely through the meadows,
    NO TRESPASSING;
When I'm tired, to lean my head on a tree,
    KEEP OFF THE GRASS;
To wander aimlessly through the woods,
    STAY ON PATHS;
For us all to gather and turn on,
    NO SMOKING;
To lie in the fields and make love,
    SEX LAWS;
To sing and raise my head and laugh at the sun,
    DISTURBING THE PEACE;
But we, the love generation, will change all this,
    FOR OUR SONS.
My son will run freely through the meadows,
    BECAUSE OF US.

---

[7] London 1961, p. 659.

My son will lean his weary head on a tree,
    SLEEP PEACEFULLY.
He'll wander aimlessly through the woods,
    HIS OWN PATH.
He'll gather with others and turn on,
    LEGALLY.
He'll lie in the fields making love,
    FREE LOVE.
My son will sing and raise his head and laugh
                               at the sun
    THIS IS WHERE IT'S AT.

What is pathetic about the foregoing (and in my experience it represents the feelings of a large number of American university students, and is the theme of countless 'pop' lyrics) is its total and mindless lack of logic, amounting to crass irresponsibility. The simplistic suggestion that all laws and inhibitions are merely the result of a desire to irritate and provoke the young, the confident assertion that a future generation will *effortlessly* inherit and inhabit a latter-day Garden of Eden, scarcely coincides with the evidence presented earlier in this book, and while sympathizing with the anonymous author's *desire* for a simpler, less aggressive society, I fear that his solution if unchallenged is much more likely to lead to a Hobbesian 'war of all against all'.

What is really extraordinary is that such sentiments should gain credence and widespread acceptance in a century which, more than any other, has produced abundant evidence of what men can and will do if unchecked by the restraints of what used to be regarded as civilized values, and by the possibility of eventual accountability not to other men but to a Creator. (Moreover, the physical manifestations of the sentiments expressed in the poem – rock festivals and other such events – although on the whole peaceful, scarcely reveal what one might describe as a genuine reverence for nature.)

Some cultural historians have claimed to see a close parallel between the situation in the West today and that prevailing in Rome during the period of Imperial decline. Despite certain unprecedented phenomena, such as the mass-proliferation of entertainment, information and propaganda, personally I see a far greater similarity between our present cultural and political situation and that prevailing in Western Europe during the closing decades of the eighteenth century. Then, too, philosophies of instinct were rampant. These included a belief in the 'noble savage', in the perfectibility of man and in the superiority of the senses to the intellect. Blake summed up the essential mood of the Romantic movement – 'Sooner murder an infant in its cradle than nurse unacted desires.'

As I have already suggested, something occurred in the years between 1750 and 1800 from which we have never really recovered; and which has resulted in an increasing polarization between the kinds of mind which first brought about industrialization on the one hand and, on the other, romanticism – 'the light that never was, on sea or land' – with its seemingly inseparable partner, revolution. The cults of romanticism and revolution both spring from a persistent youthful impatience with things as they are, allied to a naïvely optimistic (because untried and unexperienced) view of the enduring strengths and equally enduring weaknesses inherent in human nature.

The writers and *philosophes* who prepared the ground for the French Revolution, men such as Voltaire, Diderot and, to a certain extent, Rousseau, based their arguments against injustice on Reason. Yet when these ideas were translated into *action*, the dominant mood was emotional. 'Liberty, Equality and Fraternity' was a slogan designed to appeal to men's hearts rather than to their rational faculties, and, as power passed more and more from the moderates to the extremists, the shift was complete, mob-rule being eventually, of course, replaced by the inevitable strong man, Napoleon.

A curiously similar situation exists in the contemporary entertainment industry – the modern equivalent of the *philosophes,* but with one difference; it is here that the twin polarities of our age meet and fuse. Nothing could be more *rational* than the calculating intelligence that sees the dollar or sterling worth of the Beatles, of *Hair,* or the memoirs of Che Guevara syndicated throughout the capitalist presses and publishing houses of the Western world. Yet the result of this cold, calculating intelligence *could* be the same as it was in 1791 and 1792 – an unleashing of demonic energies over which the rationalist instigators would have no control and of which, if they have any sense of history, they should beware. Revolutions have an unfortunate, Oedipal tendency to destroy their own begetters.

Writing of the literary Romantic movement which began

in the 1740's,[8] gained strength with Wordsworth's and Coleridge's *Lyrical Ballads* of 1798 and is reaching its apex in the contemporary arts, G. Chatterton-Hill wrote : 'It spells anarchy in every domain . . . a systematic hostility to everyone invested with any particle of social authority – husband, or *paterfamilias,* policeman or magistrate, priest or Cabinet Minister.'

And this brings us to the crux of the whole problem. Are we faced with the impossible choice of *dehumanization* on the one hand, symbolized by the computerized society, slab-architecture and biological tamperings with the modality of human consciousness, and *subhumanization* on the other, springing from totally unbridled lusts and passions, the products of supra-egotism, devoid of any religious faith, shorn of deference, of awe, and worship, of God, man and nature?[9] Is there a way out of the *impasse* and if so where do I, as an educator, stand? At the university at which I teach, I have lately given at the beginning of each of my lecture courses on literature, a personal *credo* lasting no more than ten or fifteen minutes. In retrospect I am certain that this helped my students to guard against indoctrination, intentional or otherwise; more than that, it also helped me to clarify my own beliefs and to recognize the prejudices which underlie all systems (or even non-systems) of thought, whether derived from rationalism or emotionalism. I am certain that what follows will be coloured by that *credo,* but I have honestly sought to obviate prejudice so far as possible and to suggest ways in which education, shorn of some of the contemporary shibboleths which surround it, can assist us in regaining a sense of a future; a future designed not exclusively for the young or the old or the middle-aged, the rich, the poor or those in between, but for the community as a whole; a society in which, given the manifest limitations of human nature, men and women can live lives, not of unimaginable bliss (for that is not possible nor even probably

---

[8] Specifically, in my opinion, with Joseph Wharton's *The Enthusiast,* (1744).

[9] In *Democracy in America,* Alexis de Tocqueville suggests that 'democracy diverts the imagination from all that is external to man and fixes it on man alone.' It is interesting to reflect on the implications of these words, taken in conjunction with Lynn White's statement quoted later in Chapter VI: 'The issue is whether a democratised world can survive its own implications.'

desirable) but at least, of comparative contentment, without forfeiting their humanity.[10]

---

[10] It was not until a few years ago that I came to understand fully the meaning of the following lines in Pope's *Essay on Man*:

Know thy own point: This kind, this due degree
Of blindness, weakness, Heaven bestows on Thee.
Submit – In this, or any other sphere,
Secure to be as blest as thou canst bear [My italics]

Epistle 1. 283–286

What Pope means, in the final line, is that were men and women endowed with a guarantee, at birth, of a life totally devoid of stress, pain, unhappiness or any of the others ills which beset us, then life would be intolerably boring and uneventful; moreover, we would not be able to relish even the absence of such things. It is salutary, too, to remember that these sentiments were expressed by a man who suffered from curvature of the spine (in maturity he was only four foot six inches tall), chronic headaches, asthma, and who referred to that 'long disease, my life'. Under these circumstances it is obviously a mistake to assume, as some critics have done, that the attitudes revealed in the *Essay on Man* are smug and self-satisfied.

CHAPTER V

High Living and Plain Thinking

───────◆───────

As long as man lives in the world, he will need the
perspective and attitude of the scientist; but to the
extent that he has created the world he lives in, feels
responsible for it and has a concern for its destiny,
which is also his own destiny, he will need the perspective and attitude of the humanist.
NORTHROP FRYE: *The Stubborn Structure*

───────◆───────

As I have suggested, the philosophic and educational theorists
of the present age tend to assume that 'discussion' is in-
disputably a good thing and that it is almost magically
endowed with a virtue all its own. Therefore, the more
children can be taught to disagree about everything, the more
active their brains must be. However, Walter Bagehot, the
nineteenth-century political thinker, described 'an age of discussion' as being one in which 'the cake of custom, the
chief *preserving* force in a society, has been broken.'

What we are witnessing today is not merely an age of
discussion but one of dissolution, manifested in growing
factionalism and pettiness. It is a critical period in which loud
disputes are accompanied by generally weak conclusions.
Diagnosticians abound, but one looks, seemingly in vain, for
anyone prepared to *prescribe* for the social, political and educational maladies becoming daily more apparent. Instead
of the present hiatus and turmoil which characterize the
contemporary scene, I am making bold to suggest (and no
doubt will be attacked from some quarters for it) that there
is an urgent need for some educational theory which will
be seen to be axiomatic; something comparable to a Euclidean
theorem in geometry and something to which all men and
women of good will and good sense will be prepared to give
their assent, and, thereafter, their whole-hearted effort and

allegiance.[1] With this end in view may I tentatively suggest that the *survival* of the species is paramount and supersedes, or should supersede, all factional or other priorities.

Firstly, therefore, I am proposing the total de-politicization of our educational systems. Politics, as presently conceived and executed, is the poor man's philosophy and the following lines from Goldsmith's *The Traveller* (1765) reflect a truth which is increasingly overlooked :

> How small of all that human hearts endure,
> That part which laws or kings can cause or cure,
> Still ourselves in every place consigned,
> Our own felicity we make or find.[2]

Governments and politicians may fulfil a useful function in allowing us to externalize our feelings of frustration and anger, providing the populace at large with a convenient scapegoat on which to vent such various vexations as the unhappiness of a love-affair, the failure of a business or of the morning porridge, but insofar as politics consists of the art of promising, and occasionally providing the people with more and more materialistic benefits and increasing faction-alism, its aims and motives should be questioned. (The same stricture, of course, applies equally to commercial television and radio.) 'The evils of the world', wrote Livingstone, 'do not come, except in a minor degree from bad political machinery and will not be cured by improving it. There is a truer philosophy in the Epistle of St. James. "From whence," he asks, "come wars and fighting among you?" . . . Man is the real problem, the old, the modern problem; for the new world is not so new; humanity changes its clothes but not its nature; Adam puts on a more elaborate and complicated dress but remains the old Adam.'[3]

Anyone with a logical mind can clearly see that a *finite* world cannot go on meeting indefinitely the demands of often artificially fanned *infinite* aspirations and materialistic desires.

---

[1] I am aware that the 'truths' of plane geometry depend upon a non-existent flat surface. Nevertheless, for centuries (until Reimannian geometry in the 19th century) Euclid was regarded as virtually unassailable, and it is in this sense that I am using his work as an example.

[2] Johnson, whose truthfulness is scarcely open to doubt, claimed that he had written the conclusion of *The Traveller* in which this passage occurs.

[3] *Some Tasks for Education,* pp. 20, 22.

Today's luxuries become indiscernibly tomorrow's 'necessities', and such is the nature of Man that no sooner has one ambition been gratified than he has to invent some further object on which to fasten his want. 'Some desire' wrote Johnson in *Rasselas* (1759) 'is necessary to keep life in motion, and he, whose real wants are supplied, must admit those of fancy'; in other words 'want' is a constant, but its projections vary from a bowl of rice to an original Velasquez. Recently, I suggested on a television programme based on the theme 'Why Progress?' that the present-day inhabitant of the most modest suburban house (or even, in Britain, of a council-house) enjoys, in terms of heating, lighting, preparation and variety of food, sanitation, and other materialistic goods, a higher standard of living that did a Tudor monarch, such as Henry VIII, or early American presidents such as Washington or Jefferson. In other words, at what point does 'need' cease and greed (however understandably) take over? (Lest I be accused at this stage of exhibiting a *de haut en bas* attitude, I must state that I have never owned a stock, share, or house; that I drive a small car and have only a minimal bank-balance.) The Miltonic ideal of 'plain living and high thinking' seems increasingly, in the twentieth century, to have been inverted as society portrays a marked preference for high living coupled with plain thinking.

Mr. Escot, a character in Peacock's novel *Headlong Hall* (1816) summarized the whole dreary process of unalloyed materialism when he spoke as follows :

These improvements, as you call them, appear to me only so many links in the great chain of corruption, which will soon fetter the whole human race in irreparable slavery and incurable wretchedness.

Your improvements proceed in a simple ratio, while the factitious wants and unnatural appetites they engender proceed in a compound one; and thus one generation acquires 50 wants, and 50 means of supplying them are invented, which each in turn engenders two new ones; so that the next generation has 100, the next 200, the next 400 till every human being becomes such a helpless compound of perverted inclinations that he is altogether at the mercy of external circumstances, loses all independence and single-ness of character and degenerates so rapidly from the primi-tive dignity of his sylvan origin, that it is scarcely possible to indulge in any other expectation than that the whole species must at length be exterminated by its own infinite imbecility and vileness.

If we are to escape from the materialistic slavery envisioned in the foregoing, then we should surely begin with education. Everyone, in Western countries at least, attends school, and there learns certain rudimentary skills, basically reading, writing and mathematics. It may seem too obvious to mention, but without a knowledge of these, it would be impossible to become an engineer or scientist, statesman or physician, computer-programmer or veterinary surgeon. In other words, schools and teachers are not luxuries but their continued existence is essential in that they are the transmitters not only of our civilization but also of the written word, without which society as we know it would cease. When people write of a post-literate society (and to do so has the same absence of logic as a solipsist announcing his beliefs to *other* people) in which values, information and skills will be transmitted exclusively by television, radio, and computer, they overlook the written script without which (at the moment at least) little but talk-shows are possible. There is already a consensus among educators regarding the desirability of passing on these basic skills to all children regardless of any later specialized direction their studies may take, although there is continuing disagreement about the methods by which such skills should be inculcated. In other words, there is almost total agreement that literacy and numeracy are desirable goals for all.

I should like to hope one can obtain a similar total agreement that the survival of the species is, or ought to be, paramount, and if so that we should attempt to produce a generation whose aims are cultural rather than material, and wherein the individual is prepared to a certain and reasonable extent to subordinate his own egotistical desires and ambitions in favour of the common weal. Such an attitude does prevail in countries during times of war when a common and clearly definable purpose is evident and a sense of crisis permeates men and women of all classes. That there is a growing environmental crisis is becoming almost daily more apparent, but there seems as yet little sense of co-operation among nations or individuals to meet this with appropriate actions or attitudes. Almost daily, on television and in the national press, evidence of this crisis is manifest. Now the Cornish coast is menaced by oil pollution from an enormous tanker, or the 'red tide' threatens the fishermen of Maine; elderly persons are evicted from the only home they have ever known to make way for a motorway; an ancient building, despite all efforts by preservation societies, is razed to the ground; agricultural land is swallowed up for featureless box-like housing and countless thousand Londoners annually are subject to 'relocation'. All the victims of these and innumerable other ravages of 'progress' are acutely aware of the symptoms of the disease, but seem unaware of its essential cause. Meanwhile, politicians in various countries announce that the 'real' standard of living has risen, but neglect to take into account the declining assets in terms of unspoilt countryside, pleasant cities and villages, pure air and mental health. J. W. M. Thompson dramatized the issue in a recent article when he wrote :

> Picture the alarm there would be if every year brought a reduction in the stock of cars or factories, or in the supply of education or welfare. . . . What if there were anxious local preservation societies trying to save a power station or public library from decay or the bulldozer? It sounds ludicrous yet it is, of course, a precise, accurate picture of the fate of our environmental assets, which are equally a part of the national patrimony. . . . Hence the bleak truth that, as we grow richer, we live in increasing ugliness. Pre-industrial man, believing that more wealth naturally meant more beauty, would have marvelled at such a conjunction. It is the peculiar achievement of the modern world to have reversed the process.[4]

In twentieth-century terms this is simply a restatement of Goldsmith's lines from *The Deserted Village* :

> Ill fares the land, to hastening ills a prey
> Where wealth accumulates and men decay.

Unless we believe this state of affairs to be irremediable, then educationally certain *values* as well as facts should be included in the curriculum at all levels. No doubt objections will be raised against this proposal and those who advocate it will be accused of authoritarianism and 'brainwashing'. To such allegations I would reply as follows. Firstly, as I have already suggested, the aim of our educational system for the past half-century has been increasingly to provoke the individual mind into thought, to foment discussion of, and indeed, dissent from, previously held doctrines and dogmas. Over the same period, the conviction has steadily grown that *harmony* between nations is the indispensable pre-requisite for man's continued existence on this planet. The supra-individualism of our educational goals, however, scarcely coincides with the social consensus on a global scale to which, nominally, we are committed. Logically, either such a con-sensus is obtained or else we drift in endless 'discussion' to-wards the inevitable destruction of the entire planet as a life-supporting system.

Secondly, World War II, in addition to the hideous slaughter and mass destruction of much that was precious, left an additional cruel legacy which has paralysed much of subse-quent thought. Because the Nazi régime was authoritarian, an increasing rejection of *all* authority has resulted, no matter how benevolently inspired or exercised, and anyone who attempts to exercise control is facilely, but damagingly, accused of 'fascism'. However, as Edmund Burke wrote in 'Thoughts on French Affairs' (1791):

> Men are qualified for civil liberty in exact proportion to their disposition to put moral chains upon their own ap-petites. . . . Society cannot exist unless a controlling power upon will and appetite be placed somewhere, and the less of it there is within, the more there is without. It is ordained in the eternal constitution of things that men of intemperate minds cannot be free. Their passions forge their fetters.

Although Burke is referring specifically to political freedom and responsibility, his words have a far wider application in a cybernetic age. Are machines in the process of enslaving mankind both by creating a void where there was once a pride in accurate work and in imaginative and fair administra-tion, and also by an absolute, unquestionable authority? Is man capable of disciplining his own artificially-created 'wants', or will he intemperately and self-indulgently proceed with the rape of this planet (his only home) resulting in that state of 'incurable wretchedness' envisioned by Mr. Escot?

Ortega Y Gasset in *The Revolt of the Masses* observes that it has become 'impossible to do more than instruct the masses in the technique of modern life; it has been found impossible to educate them . . . They have been given tools for an intenser form of existence, but no feelings for their great historic duties.'[5] If we are to survive, *someone, soon, somewhere,* must attempt the diversion to cultural goals which I have suggested above, and if this does not come about as a result of individual self-control (and this can only ensue as a result of educating people to the full implications of their actions) then such control will either be obtained through a benevolent form of despotism or, if left too late, through a malevolent one.

'Education', wrote Ruskin, 'does not mean teaching people to know what they do not know, it means teaching them to behave as they do not behave.' Surely, even at primary level, children can be taught to recognize the interdependence of all things in nature, or as Pope expressed it :

> From Nature's chain whatever link you strike,
> Tenth or ten thousandth, breaks the chain alike.[6]

From this it is only a short step to creating a morality based upon survival not only of the individual but of the species. It is significant that this would by no means result in a new Morality'. Of the Seven Deadly Sins, only sloth possibly would be seen to be environmentally neutral and even this, if it results in the mindless inactivity (accidie) revealed in the poem *For My Son* quoted in the previous chapter, is not above censure. The remaining six would still stand. Lust, despite all birth-control measures, is manifestly an undesirable quality in today's overcrowded world; pride, as indicated earlier, results in man's unthinking dominion *over* nature instead of a humbler, more harmonious relationship; envy and avarice bring about a state in which each person wants an *increasing* share in a cake which, comparatively speaking, is diminishing; gluttony in a world facing food and water shortages is manifestly 'sinful', while anger, because it clouds one's mind and results in a tendency towards simplistic solutions to complex problems and a denial of a logical approach, is inimical to a sane or just solution of human ills.

---

[5] It is interesting to compare the above with the following by T. S. Eliot, who saw that 'the tendency of unlimited industrialism is to create masses of men and women detached from tradition, alienated from religion and susceptible to suggestions: in other words, a mob.' And a mob, he adds, 'will be no less a mob if it is well-fed, well-housed and well-disciplined.'

[6] *Essay on Man,* I, 245–246.

C

The so-called 'New Morality', in that it encourages and enlarges the mass-ego is, not just in subjective terms, as great a threat as the reductionism and homunculism which are the products of what Taylor calls 'technomania'. Nor should the 'liberal', humanistic mentality be unaware that in its largely matristic attitude it, too, may derive a great deal of its flexibility and tolerance from both distance (i.e. removal from reality) and sloth. Writing of the 'universal culture' which he saw as one of the characteristics of the twentieth century, George Santayana, defining it as 'always tolerant, always fluid, smiling on everything exotic and on everything new', declared it to be 'a sin against the principle of life itself'. 'If the humanist,' he added, 'could really live up to his ancient maxim, *humani nil a me alienum puto,* (I count nothing human indifferent to me) he would sink into moral anarchy and artistic impotence – the very things from which our liberal, romantic world is so greatly suffering.'[7]

Perhaps it ought to be made clear at this point that I am not proposing something tantamount or comparable to Illich's 'de-schooling'. His ideas certainly do posit a challenge to all those interested not merely in education but in the political and social implications of his writings. However, like so many radical suggestions, they do contain a fatal flaw – Illich himself is a product of an educational system which, whatever its manifest deficiencies may be, has given him his sense of 'concern' without which he would not have been moved to voice his thoughts or attempt to disseminate his viewpoint. What I am suggesting could perhaps be described as 'reschooling', an educational shift in emphasis at primary level not hopefully at the expense of formal learning, but with the axiomatic purpose of survival serving as a framework within which other academic and cultural activities could take place.

Of course, such a programme is strewn with dangers and difficulties, but the alternatives appear to be so evidently and irreversibly fatal that it would seem that if we are to heed the plea contained in 'A Blueprint for Survival'[8] that 'as soon as the best means of inculcating the values of the stable society have been agreed upon, they should be incorporated into our educational systems', then the sooner such values can be

---

[7] *The Genteel Tradition at Bay* (New York, 1931), pp. 7, 8.
[8] *The Ecologist,* January, 1972.

determined the better. Meanwhile, simple logic dictates that certain values are deleterious to mankind both individually and collectively; in an environmental context the words of Pascal have a significance additional to that normally ascribed to them : 'It is the nature of man to believe and to love; if he has not the right objects for his belief and love, he will attach himself to wrong ones.'

Having proposed that education at primary level could inculcate such 'right objects' for belief and that such 'right objects' should be both life-enhancing and life-supporting, I shall next consider and suggest how other levels of education could adapt themselves to meet some of the challenges outlined above, without forfeiting their historic roles or discarding their very necessary standards.

CHAPTER VI

Education for What?

———◆———

By making education the slave of scholarship, the
university has renounced its responsibility to human
culture and its old, proud claim to possess, as educator and moulder of men, an *ecumenical* function.
It has disowned in short what teaching has always
meant; a care and concern for the future of man, a
Platonic love of the species, not for what it is, but
what it might be.

PROFESSOR WILLIAM ARROWSMITH

———◆———

An increasing number of 'young' people between the ages of
sixteen and fifty-five appears to be turning towards philosophies of instinct, an 'impressionistic' attitude to life and, at
least among students in the Humanities, towards their studies;
to an embracing of the occult, the exotic, the bizarre. Their
attitude to the curriculum is, as the sociologist Robert Nisbet
suggests, very similar to the way that 'sacraments and liturgy
were regarded by early, zealous Protestants: unnecessary to
those with grace and unavailing to those without.'[1] Commenting on such earlier zealots, Dryden wrote in *Religio Laici*
(1682):

> The tender page with horny fist was gall'd
> And he was gifted most that loudest bawl'd:
> The spirit gave the doctoral degree . . .
> Study and pains were now no more their care;
> Texts were explain'd by fasting and by prayer;
>
> 404–406; 413–414

If one substitutes drug-taking and transcendental meditation
for fasting and prayer, Dryden's description is a remarkably
up-to-date one of contemporary attitudes prevalent on many

———

[1] *The Degradation of the Academic Dogma: The University in
America*, 1945–1970. (New York 1971).

campuses, particularly in the United States.[2] The staggering growth of interest in Oriental philosophy and religion, with their emphasis on quietism and theosophy, is another manifestation of this swing away from traditional Western ways of thought and particularly reflects a rejection of the truths to be reached through logical thought. I have already suggested that we are currently experiencing a wave of neo-romanticism which, for reasons which will emerge, I find both hopeful and at the same time profoundly disquieting, and it is interesting to compare contemporary youthful attitudes with the following from a letter written by the poet, John Keats, to his friend Benjamin Bailey on 22 November, 1817:

> I am certain of nothing but of the holiness of the Heart's affections and the truth of Imagination – What the Imagination seizes as Beauty must be Truth – whether it existed before or not – for I have the same idea of all our passions as of love they are all in their sublime, creative of essential Beauty. . . . The Imagination may be compared to Adam's dream – he awoke and found it truth. I am the more zealous in this affair, because I have never yet been able to perceive how any thing can be known for truth by consequitive [sic] reasoning – and yet it must be. Can it be that even the greatest philosopher ever arrived at his goal without putting aside numerous objections. However it may be, *O for a life of sensations rather than of thoughts!* [My italics]

The insistence in the foregoing of the imagination as being the sole vehicle of truth, coupled with the rejection of logic ('consequitive reasoning'), and indeed punctuation, must strike a responsive chord to one living in the modern world but, as I have indicated earlier, such an attitude, however understandable and praiseworthy in art or music, can be catastrophic if transferred to the realm of practical affairs. Matthew Arnold foresaw this danger when he wrote:

> Ideas cannot be too much prized in and for themselves, cannot be too much lived with; but to transport them abruptly into the world of politics and practice, violently to revolutionize this world to their bidding – that is quite another thing. There is the world of ideas and there is the world of practice.

---

[2] I have examined this phenomenon at some length in 'The New Impuritans', in *Education: Threatened Standards* (London, 1972).

Shelley, Keats's contemporary, tried in his younger days to revolutionize society to his own bidding and was naïvely appalled that mankind did not docilely accept what today would be called his life-style. Oxford University found *one* Shelley too much and expelled him in his first year for a somewhat self-conscious attempt to advertise his pamphlet, *The Necessity of Atheism*. Today, on many campuses, one is faced with a whole generation of Shelleys, each member distinguished by a brand of individualism which appears to feel threatened unless it is constantly harped upon. In the presence of such, the thoughts that persistently haunt my mind are : does this rejection of logic betoken a *fear* of thought? Is it perhaps due to a subconscious feeling that it is all too late for a logical solution to the overwhelming problems which beset us on all sides? If so, does it betoken what C. P. Snow predicted in his talk at Westminster College, Missouri in 1968 (to which I referred in the first chapter) and which he described as 'enclave-making', a drawing of the curtains of the mind? Unfashionable though it may be, I am suggesting that never has there been such a need for a revival, not of feeling (there is an abundance of that among youth), but of the logical thought-processes and their subsequent application to contemporary problems. 'A man' wrote Dryden 'is to be cheated into passion, but be reason'd into Truth.' It should then emerge that one cannot have A *and* B, if A is diametrically opposed to B. It is obvious, for example, that one cannot be in favour of total, unbridled freedom and at the same time support the necessity for strict regulations to ensure clean air, pure water and an environment fit for human life. It is equally illogical to clamour for 'justice' while at the same time engaging in a doctrinaire repudiation and denigration of authority, symbolized by the police, the sole guardians of anyone's rights and the only bulwark against the *bellum omnium contra omnes*. (Even the conventional alliance between anti-war and anti-pollution groups may perhaps be an illogical one in the light of a growing awareness of the equation between population and pollution which has given rise in the United States to the bastardized term 'popullution'.)

It must also be obvious that permissiveness cannot be canonized as an isolated phenomenon confined to the theatre, cinema, television and the arts in general. It clearly infiltrates all spheres of human affairs and if one can 'do one's own thing' with impunity in film-production, to take an isolated example, then does not the same heedless and unthinking ethic also apply to a firm which 'does its own thing', polluting a river, destroying a community or dismissing a work force merely because it does not meet its self-appointed standards of 'performance' (the pun is intentional)? This is basically the same point that C. S. Lewis makes in *God in The Dock:*

> Though the 'right to happiness' is chiefly claimed for the sexual impulse, it seems to me impossible that the matter should stay there. The fatal principle, once allowed in that department, must sooner or later seep through our whole lives. We thus advance towards a state of society in which not only each man but every impulse in each man claims carte blanche. And then . . . our civilization will have died at heart, and will – one dare not even add 'unfortunately' – be swept away.[3]

Of much greater significance than all the foregoing is the logical alternative between technology and democracy. Can men have both, or is this another manifestation of the eternal desire to have one's cake and eat it? In an article entitled 'The Historical Roots of our Ecological Crisis', Professor Lynn White, writing of the relationship between science and technology, makes the following observations :

> Science was traditionally aristocratic, speculative, intellectual in intent; technology was lower-class, empirical, *action-oriented*. The quite sudden fusion of these two, towards the middle of the nineteenth century, is surely related to the slightly prior and contemporary democratic revolutions which, by reducing social barriers, tended to assert a functional unity of brain and hand. . . . *The issue is whether a democratized world can survive its own implications.*[4] [My italics]

Examples of the force of White's statement are already apparent and daily becoming more evident.

Motor cars, when they were confined to a privileged minority, posed no serious threat to the environment either in terms of exhaust pollution, destruction of houses to facilitate the building of new roads (obsolescent almost as soon as completed), or in a serious depletion of natural resources. With a

---

[3] Michigan, 1970, p. 322.
[4] *The Environmental Handbook,* ed. Garrett de Bell, New York 1970, p. 45.

burgeoning population, growing affluence, coupled with the technique of mass-production (a classic example of technology) and an increasing tendency for families to gravitate from need to greed, and own two, three or even four cars, the motor car has, in my own life-time, been transformed from a quick and convenient method of travel to a Frankenstein monster before which all other considerations have to yield. Demonstrably the indefinite proliferation of cars cannot continue and some method of control will be evolved. The present tendency in London, Paris, New York and other great cities to make it increasingly expensive to use parking facilities is scarcely consonant with democracy, but a 'democratic' solution, involving such expedients as lotteries for car-ownership, has never been mooted simply because such a solution would result in manifest absurdities.

To cite just one other example, medical technology has now made it possible for human beings to be 'frozen' after death in the hope that at some future date, the cause of their death may be eliminated and they may be revived to 'enjoy' life once again. Leaving aside the more macabre aspects of this Rip Van Winkle experiment (and one cannot but wonder how long Thomas Jefferson, for example, would stay sane if such facilities had existed in the early nineteenth century and were he to be revivified into the breathless pace of New York City in the 1970s) one thing has clearly emerged and that is that any such process is not, and probably never will be, available on a mass basis. The cost is prohibitive to all but the extremely rich, and this is true of a growing number of recent technological productions ranging from the Concorde aircraft and Apollo space-ships to kidney machines and heart-transplants.

Conversely, it is both logical and feasible to conceive of a democratic society existing in a rural area, based on a largely agrarian economy, every person and family being provided with a sufficiency of land on which to produce food for their own immediate wants, together with a modest cash crop for sale at a local market. Such an idyllic state (if that is what is desired) will not come about overnight, and in Britain at least would necessitate a considerable reduction in the present population and would certainly not automatically be a natural outgrowth of the destruction or demise of capitalism. If we genuinely want what Taylor describes as a 'paraprimitive solution' then, however *passionately* we may desire it, the necessary means to achieve it will have to be worked out in a logical manner.[5]

Moreover, since almost all thinking people are convinced by now that society cannot continue its heedless, *laissez-faire* attitude towards the crucial questions of the day, should not courses, or at least a course, in logic be made a compulsory pre-requisite for entry into all the professions, ensuring that architects, engineers, scientists, doctors, lawyers, politicians and above all, teachers are made aware of the impact of their actions and words, not just on a section of the community, nor yet even on a nation, but in the perspective of a world in which instant communications and almost instant travel are, whether we like it or not, creating an interdependence formerly associated with the boroughs that constitute the cities of London and New York? Do we, for example, really want to encourage children and students (through subsidized fares) to acquire an appetite for *air*-travel when we know that a four-engined jet-aircraft in normal flight apart from its enormous consumption of natural resources emits approximately two and two-thirds tons of carbon dioxide and one and one-third tons of water vapour every ten minutes? Moreover, if the experience of traffic and road-space is typical, we should even now, given the concurrent rises in population and affluence, be pondering the siting of not just the *third* London airport but that of the fourth, fifth, sixth or seventh, and indeed why stop there? Simply because international tourism is lucrative (and even this is now being challenged) does not, alas, mean that it is life-enhancing or consonant with survival. Any economic or other system which forgets that its values are predicated on a continuing human intelligence capable of appreciating its 'benefits' is either ill-taught in basic logic or else criminally insane.

Also, surveying the throngs progressing through an Oxford or Cambridge college on a typical summer day, or trooping through Westminster Abbey or the Louvre, is it heretical to remember Matthew Arnold's reactions to the new railway line between Islington and Camberwell? 'Of what use' he asked, is such a line if it simply enables one 'to pass from a dismal and illiberal life in Islington to a dismal and illiberal life in Camberwell?' Movement is supplanting travel and by

---

[5] Although I do not agree *totally* with all its recommendations, 'A Blueprint for Survival' is an excellent example of such a combination of passion and logic.

C*

movement I mean the mass transportation of the type of mentality exemplified by Cardinal Newman's 'sailors'; they move around the world, seeing many strange and exotic sights 'but the multiplicity of external objects, which they have encountered, forms no symmetrical and consistent picture upon their imagination; they see the tapestry of human life, as it were on the wrong side and it tells no story.'[6] They return home unchanged, unaffected and basically as ignorant as when they left their home port, simply because one cannot derive anything from an experience unless one's own mind is educated and open, so that in Newman's phrase eventually the 'objects of our knowledge' are made 'subjectively our own'.

Speed and innovation have become increasingly the emperatives of the twentieth century and referring to this John Howard asks the following question :

Why should anyone presume that newness, *per se*, is to be equated with worthiness? Why is that which is different automatically regarded as an improvement?

One has only to view a child tiring of a brand-new toy and avidly grasping for yet another one to realize the answer to Howard's questions, and it is significant that the romantic temper with its emphasis upon the supremacy of feeling over thought has a perpetual tendency to canonize childhood. Wordsworth, for example, in the *Immortality Ode* (1802–1804) addresses a 'six-years darling of a pygmy size' in a flattering apostrophe which unfortunately lacks only the possibility of comprehension on behalf of its recipient to give it a superficial (if pre-Freudian) impressiveness :

Thou, whose exterior semblance doth belie
Thy soul's immensity;
Thou best philosopher, who dost keep
Thy heritage, thou eye among the blind,
That, deaf and silent, reads't the eternal deep,
Haunted forever by the eternal mind.

(109–114)

Much the same sentiments permeate Blake's *Song of Innocence* and *Songs of Experience,* but this same matristic preoccupation with childhood, if it results in a desire to inculcate and preserve 'childishness' on a materialistic plane, needs to

---

[6] *The Idea of a University* (New York, 1964), Discourse V, p. 102.

be questioned and repudiated. This is particularly true of the United States, a country which has ridden on a surge of supra-individualism and romanticism ever since it founding, and which is today, more than ever, in technological terms the pace-setter for the rest of the world.

Returning to the educational scene, the following by John Jay Chapman is today even more perceptive and pertinent than ever :

> The young person . . . during the past quarter century has been like a rat in a bag which the rat-catcher keeps agitating lest the creature's teeth get a purchase on the prison. The . . . youth cannot be expected to get hold of any idea while the kaleidoscope is turning so furiously. He is numb and dizzy. He cannot connect his reading with his environment; for the books of the world have been projected out of quietude. They reflect stability, depth, relaxation, and all those conditions of peace and harmony which make thought possible. The youth, therefore, discards books as incomprehensible – foolish in fact. Education has for the time being lost its significance.

Some readers concede that 'book-learning' has suffered an eclipse, but would assert that television now can, and increasingly does, educate the young. Leaving aside for the moment such strictly academic programmes as the Open University in Britain, television emphatically does *not* inculcate a logical concept of human affairs, but serves rather to cater to a succession of evanescent and conflicting emotions. One can pass in a single evening through a whole gamut of feelings ranging from indignation at the plight of the Vietnamese war-orphans or the homeless in London or Chicago, to amusement at some trivial situation-comedy, interest and either agreement or disagreement with a guest on a discussion programme; then a final late-night film and so to bed. The description of 'seafaring men' in Newman's *The Idea of a University* to which I previously alluded in this chapter is so applicable to the average television-viewer that I cannot resist quoting it again and at greater length :

> [They] range from one end of the earth to the other; but the multiplicity of external objects, which they have encountered, forms no symmetrical and consistent picture upon their imagination; they see the tapestry of human life, as it were on the wrong side, and it tells no story. They sleep and they rise up and they find themselves, now in

Europe, now in Asia; they see visions of great cities and
wild regions; they are in the marts of commerce, or amid
the islands of the South; they gaze on Pompey's Pillar, or
on the Andes; and nothing which meets them carries them
forward or backward, to any idea beyond itself. Nothing
has a drift or relation; nothing has a history or a promise
. . . Perhaps you are near such a man on a particular
occasion, and expect him to be shocked or perplexed at
something which occurs; but one thing is much the same
to him as another, or, if he is perplexed, it is as not knowing
what to say, whether it is right to admire, or to ridicule, or
to disapprove, while conscious that some expression of
opinion is expected from him; for in fact he has no standard
of judgement at all, and no landmarks to guide him to a
conclusion. Such is mere acquisition, and . . . no one
would dream of calling it philosophy. (pp. 102–103).

Another example of the unity of the age is the escalating
trend over the past two or three decades in the teaching of
modern languages. Until approximately 1950, French, German, Italian and other living languages were taught in very
much the same fashion and with much the same aim as were
Latin and Greek. Instruction was formal and was directed
at enabling the pupil, after five or six years, to read the poets,
novelists, dramatists and philosophers of other countries in
the original and without recourse to translation. This was
deemed a sufficient end it itself, and even if one found it impossible to order a bath in Paris or haggle over a bill in
Rome at least one's mind could be stimulated and enlarged
by the essays of Montaigne, the poetry of Goethe and the
inspiration of Dante. Suddenly all this changed, and with
the introduction of the 'direct method' the emphasis swung
to conversational ability and, no doubt because of the proliferation of foreign travel and with Britain's recent entry into
the Common Market in mind, even more emphasis upon this
method of modern-language teaching will ensue, together with
the paraphernalia of language-laboratories and other pieces of
technological gadgetry.

I am not suggesting, of course, that it is impossible to read
both Schiller (in a bath!) and the menus in Bonn restaurants,
but simply that there has been a fairly radical shift both in
method and aim, a shift away from Newman's 'philosophy'
(the love of wisdom) to 'acquisition'; another move away from
the contemplative to the 'action-oriented' to which Lynn

White referred and which was quoted earlier in this chapter. My objections to the new method of teaching languages certainly do not arise from an unthinking prejudice or nostalgia. Quite simply, the new method involves a further dependence on electrical energy as opposed to human skills and effort, and is therefore in a small way making further demands on dwindling natural resources. Moreover, one only has to multiply ten thousandfold such small demands for the sum total to become truly formidable. Writing in the *Saturday Review,* Harvey Wheeler has expressed himself as follows:

> Ecologists tell us we shall have to mount a revolution of declining expectations. Gadgets will have to go. Creature comforts will have to give way to cultural comforts. . . . Never again will they [the people of advanced technological societies] or their children enjoy as many material conveniences. This is the real revolution implicit in the new politics of ecology.[7]

Nor should one ignore the validity of Emerson's observation when Samuel Morse sent his first message and someone remarked: 'Now Maine can talk to Florida.' 'Yes,' said Emerson, 'but has Maine anything to say to Florida?'

Ironically, the same technology which has enabled mass-movement to become, at least in Western countries, a commonplace, when translated to the sphere of building techniques and materials, is rapidly making more and more cities look the same, thereby, it would seem, eventually diminishing and weakening the appetite for 'tourism'. A suburb in Detroit, for example, is interchangeable with one in Los Angeles and even the city of London is rapidly losing the distinctive flavour it once had. It does, however, seem tragic that the cure may prove worse than the disease and surely some variety could be encouraged to prevent this drift towards an architectural peneplain.

It may be alleged that these problems are beyond the scope of educators and belong more properly in the realm of national or international politics. My main contention, however, is that *all* of today's power-wielders, including architects, politicians and those whom Taylor calls 'technomaniacs', are products of *educational* systems and that at some time they were taught to count and to read and write; but what

---

[7] 'Politics of Ecology'. March 7, 1970.

ethical values were instilled, if any? Was the cultivation of a sense of beauty and harmony absent from their studies and instruction, or were they taught to regard such qualities as irrelevant and fusty? Educators must recognize that to a great extent theirs is the responsibility for the present and future state of mankind. If they admit to being powerless and attribute a person's character and attitudes solely to a combination of genes and environment, then they might as well be honest and confess that it is of little importance what happens at schools and universities, since their products are only hastening an already catastrophic trend. In this case, Illich is the sole voice of sanity on the contemporary educational scene.

CHAPTER VII

Rediscovery

———◆———

M. JOURDAIN: What? When I say: 'Nicole, bring me my slippers, and give me my night-cap', is that prose?
PROFESSOR OF PHILOSOPHY: Yes, Sir.
M. JOURDAIN: Good Heavens! For more than forty years I have been speaking prose without knowing it.
MOLIÈRE: *Le Bourgeois Gentilhomme*, II, iv.

———◆———

Education appears, at least over the past two centuries, to have shaped itself largely in response to the demands of the society in which it has taken place. In the nineteenth century in America, for example, there were roads and railways to be built, canals to be dug and a seemingly limitless frontier to be tamed. Faced with these and countless other tasks of a technical nature, pragmatism supplanted the older ideal epitomized by the *trivium* (grammar, rhetoric and logic) and the *quadrivium* (arithmetic, astronomy, geometry and music) which, in the seventeenth and eighteenth centuries, were the educational bases at Harvard, and at the other American universities then in existence. With the establishment in the 1860s of the 'land-grant' colleges the recommendations of the Morill Act of 1862 were implemented. This Act sought to establish one college in every state for instruction in:

> such branches of learning as are related to agriculture and the mechanic arts . . . to promote liberal and practical education of the industrial classes in the several pursuits and professions of life.

Thus practicality became established as the basic norm of American higher education, and it is a natural extension of the above that has led to the establishment in recent years of courses in flower-arrangement, business administration, funeral-parlour direction and playground techniques – courses which, although they initially earned scorn, particularly from European observers, nevertheless soon became entrenched and earned (and still earn) precisely the same number of 'credits' as do courses in Shakespeare, Hegel or chemistry. All of these courses came into existence because of social demand, just as 'Black Studies' are a response to legitimate pressure from black students that Afro-American literature, history and music be recognized as worthy of academic study and recognition.

Some eight or nine years ago Stewart Udall, who was then Secretary of the Interior, gave the commencement address at the college at which I was then teaching, in which he observed that from the time of the founding of the James-town colony in the early seventeeth century, so far as Americans were concerned, every tree felled, every river dammed, every acre of ground tamed had constituted a victory. He then proceeded to argue that this whole concept has now to be reversed and that henceforth every tree, every river and every acre spared the ravages of man, should become the aim of the whole population of the United States. So far, however, apart from one or two isolated incidents such as the environmental 'teach-in' in the spring of 1970, in certain states the use of lead-free petrol, and the banning of supersonic aircraft over the continental United States (ascribed, quite wrongly, in certain quarters in Britain and France to American jealousy of the Concorde project), Udall's vision has yet to be translated into educational or political action.

In California, however, which is in a peculiar way the forerunner of so many contemporary movements (the student uprising at Berkeley was the first of many which subsequently spread throughout the Western world), a small city, appropriately named Pleasanton, whose population escalated from five thousand to thirty thousand, has decreed an absolute ban on further growth. No additional building is allowed and no land is for sale, the City Council having reached the conclusion that their present population represents an optimum in terms of education, health, sanitation and all the other amenities. Bologna in Italy, which has a communist-controlled city administration, has also decreed a growth limit of 600,000, although previous plans foresaw an expansion from the city's million. This experiment has many additional interesting present half-million inhabitants to a total of well over one facets. The historic city centre, now sadly dilapidated, will be carefully restored with the use of the same materials as those used originally. The mayor has stated that the plan is not aimed merely at halting growth, but has the positive aim of making the historic centre once again the real centre of the city's life and that his administration intends to protect it from business 'speculators', ensuring that it is inhabited by the artisans whose ancestors created it.

In contrast, it is tragically obvious to even a casual observer that the prices of cottages in most British villages precludes the remotest possibility of their being bought and owned by the original villagers, who are either being forced away or into suitably and discreetly distanced 'estates' whose drab uniformity is in striking contrast to the picturesque diversity of the village proper. This represents another victory for 'mobility' over stasis, and centuries of continuity and tradition have in the last two decades been ruthlessly and unthinkingly destroyed. If, as I believe, the experiments at Pleasanton and Bologna represent the small beginnings of a mood and an attitude which will spread, then perhaps those involved in education should prepare in advance to meet this new social demand, and indeed examine its implications and applications in some detail.

Recently, at universities, colleges and schools there has been a growing demand for 'relevance' but this has, unfortunately, too often degenerated into a philistine desire to abandon anything which is not connected directly with the 'here and now', resulting in a breathless preoccupation with the passing scene. What advocates of this persuasion are really asking for is topicality, derived from the Greek *topos*, meaning something peculiar to a specific time or place. Relevant, on the other hand, by derivation means to lift something *above* the current of contemporaneity and to connect it with distant events and larger issues. In its true sense, relevance has much in common with Newman's definition of 'a truly great intellect'. It is, he wrote, 'one which takes a connected view of old and new, past and present, far and near, and which has an insight into the influence of all these one on another . . . It possesses the knowledge, not only of things, but also of their mutual and true relations; knowledge, not merely considered as acquirement, but as philosophy.'[1]

[1] *The Idea of a University*, p. 101.

The danger of topicality is that it tends to produce short-term solutions to far-ranging problems and therefore is, of course, merely another form of pragmatism. It fails, in short, to recognize that behind the various problems which beset us is the appetitive nature of man, and thus attacks the symptoms while ignoring the basic disease.

Obviously all students cannot be great intellects, but many are capable of developing an ability to take the connected view necessary to reach an understanding of the problems confronting modern man.

If even some of the premises in what I have written up to this point are admitted, then two courses of action would seem to follow. Firstly, we should attempt to raise rather than lower the threshold of boredom. Unfortunately, through a confusion over 'wants' and 'needs', the opposite has recently occurred. An alcoholic may want a drink when he needs a cure; a child may want to play with matches when he needs to have them removed from his grasp; young people may want things which will result in satiety and boredom when they need deferred gratification so as not to risk 'blunting the fine point of pleasure'. Evidently, recent trends such as the lowering of the voting age, teenage promiscuity, the increased use and ownership of cars by the young, earlier marriages (and divorces) all conspire to bring about a tendency towards instant gratification followed by boredom and then by the need to find newer, most extravagant objects of want.[2] The drug cult may well be, in fact, not merely an act of youthful rebellion against the older generation, but also an attempt to escape from the boredom resulting from such instant gratification.

I hope that no critic is going to impute to me, as a result of the above, a dislike of the young, or a jealousy of their new-found outlets for perennial youthful hedonism. It is because I genuinely care for my students and my own children that I am challenging those who are cynically catering to (and actively enlarging) youthful aspirations and desires in order to increase their own political or economic capital; the real beneficiaries of these trends are the calculating

---

[2] I grew up in war-time Britain when, owing to petrol-rationing, a car-journey was to many of my generation a luxury. One of my own children, as familiar with Washington and New York as he is with London sulked slightly on a recent car journey because he wanted for novelty's sake to travel to his destination by train!

minds which see their own immediate advantages derived from promoting a new sartorial fashion or 'pop-star', discothèque or motor-cycle craze. A news item in the *International Herald Tribune*[3], which arrived just as I had completed the last sentence, exemplifies the foregoing so completely that it deserve inclusion here. Apparently a dozen young Japanese flew recently to Copenhagen to marry 'Danish-style'. Helmeted 'vikings' sounded bronze horns as the couples left the ceremony after the mayor had presided over the ceremony. Another hundred Japanese brides and grooms will fly to Denmark next month to indulge in a similar ceremony. One of the grooms, a twenty-four-year-old Tokyo office employee, is reported to have declared : 'It's not cheaper this way, but I always *wanted* to go to Europe and have a European honeymoon.' This may sound innocuous enough, until one reads that the cost of the journey and ceremony amounted to five thousand dollars, and one must then wonder who implanted this bizarre 'want' in his mind? It cannot conceivably be aything remotely resembling an innate need, since for countless millennia his compatriots have managed to exist, marry and breed without ever having heard of, let alone visited, Denmark. Additionally, this sort of mindless movement, unless checked or rationed, contributes, in however small a fashion, to the demand for air space, congestion on the roads leading from airports, the displacement of families to facilitate such, and all the general ills which people voice but over which increasingly they feel they have no control, although they are frequently themselves as unthinkingly guilty as the Japanese cited above. (This same stricture must unfortunately also embrace such apparently 'harmless' phenomena as the twinning of cities, international sporting events and others which result in almost incessant air travel and the consequent cumulative depletion of essential sources of energy and further depredations of the environment.) 'Evil', wrote Thomas Hood, 'is wrought by want of Thought, as well as want of Heart.'

Secondly, I would like to suggest that, given the appetitive nature of mankind and the disastrous direction in which the unbridled curiosity of the species appears to be leading us collectively and individually, we have never sufficiently investigated the possibilities of *rediscovery* in our educa-

[3] April 3, 1973.

tional programmes as an adequate substitute for discovery, and as a possible source of intellectual satisfaction. Although Molière was satirizing the bourgeois simplicity and pretensions of M. Jourdain in the epigraph at the head of this chapter, the passage nevertheless does reveal an innocent joy at his 'discovery' that all his life he had been speaking prose.

As a teacher of seventeenth- and eighteenth-century literature (and consequently of the philosophy, history and theology of those periods) I am constantly gratified and surprised at the reactions of many of today's undergraduates to the religious and philosophical theories expounded in Milton's *Paradise Lost* and Pope's *Essay on Man,* to cite just two examples. It is as if a new planet had suddenly appeared, and their intellectual excitement at such 'novel' views is both stimulating and encouraging. Of particular interest is their reaction to the belief, commonly held in the past, in the value of collective, as opposed to individual, wisdom. This is so contrary to the contemporary cult of 'doing your own thing', that it affords yet another opportunity to challenge, from an environmental and social viewpoint, the irresponsibility and cant of the current slogan.

To those who would question the relevancy of such studies I would suggest firstly that nothing is more vital to our frenzied, open-nerved culture than to recapture something of that golden mean, that emphasis upon moderate ambitions and appetites (together with the insistence that man's overweening pride was at the root of most of his problems) which the writers, theologians and philosophers of the late seventeenth and early eighteenth centuries both preached and seriously attempted, with varying degrees of success, to practise. Consider, for example, the following lines from the *Essay on Man* in relation to the present predicament of society throughout the entire world :

Go, wiser thou ! and, in thy scale of sense,
Weigh thy opinion against Providence;
Call imperfection what thou fanciest such,
Say here he[4] gives too little, there too much :
Destroy all creatures for thy sport or gust
Yet cry, if man's unhappy, God's unjust;
If man alone engross not Heaven's high care,
Alone made perfect here, immortal there :

---

[4] God, or the ultimate source of being.

Snatch from his hand the balance and the rod,
Rejudge his justice, he the God of God.
In pride, in reasoning pride, our error lies;
All quit their sphere and rush into the skies. . . .
Ask for what end the heavenly bodies shine,
Earth for whose use? Pride answers, 'Tis for mine :
For *me* kind Nature wakes her genial power,
Suckles each herb, and spreads out every flower;
Annual for *me*, the grape, the rose renew
The juice nectareous, and the balmy dew;
For *me,* the mine a thousand treasures brings
For *me*, health gushes from a thousand springs;
Seas roll to waft *me*, suns to light *me* rise;
My footstool earth, my canopy the skies.'[5]   [My italics]

In this passage the poet contemptuously indicates the ego-centricity of human nature and indicates ironically the myopic attitude of those who regard all of nature as created exclusively for their pleasure or profit, not recognizing in their folly that in the great scheme of the universal intelligence :

> Who sees with equal eye, as God of all,
> A hero perish or a sparrow fall,
> Atoms or systems into ruin hurled,
> And now a bubble burst, and now a world

man is simply a part of creation, endowed with only a *finite* intellect in an infinite cosmos. Humility would surely be a more fitting posture, exemplified by the traditional kneeling when engaged in the act of prayer. The twentieth century, however, which has almost totally repudiated God and is in the process of extirpating nature, manifests a dia-metrically opposed arrogance and in an extraordinary way, as the human predicament darkens so the arrogance, far from diminishing, appears to increase. Malcolm Muggeridge writing on the same subject expresses himself as follows :

> We cannot live without God, and when we try to, we are
> fated, either to imagine ourselves to be gods and so able to
> shape our own destiny, flying like Icarus into the sun, or to
> relapse into carnality, seeking fulfilment through the senses;
> resorting to sex, drugs and violence, and finding only satiety,
> fantasy and despair; succumbing, as what remains of
> Western civilization so evidently is, to megalomania or
> erotomania, or both.[6]

---

[5] I 113–126; 131–140.
[6] Foreword to *Trousered Apes* (New Rochelle, 1972).

Perhaps the true crisis of our own century springs from a generation which is in Aldous Huxley's words obsessed by a 'chronic sense of unappeased desires from which men naturally religious, but condemned by circumstances to have no religion, are bound to suffer.'

When I re-read Shaw's *Too True to be Good* two or three years ago, one particular passage seemed to embody so many of the spiritual and moral dilemmas which face all of us in the religious, educational and environmental spheres (and as I hope is becoming clear these three are all closely interrelated)[7] that perhaps the reader will excuse yet another quotation. The words are spoken in the play by Aubrey, the unfrocked priest :

The fatal word NOT has been miraculously inserted into all our creeds : in the desecrated temples where we knelt murmuring 'I believe' we stand with stiff knees and stiffer necks shouting 'Up, all', the erect posture is the mark of the man : let lesser creatures kneel and crawl : we will not kneel and we do not believe ! But what next? Is no enough? For a boy, yes : for a man, never. Are we any the less obsessed with a belief when we are denying it than when we were affirming it? No : I must have affirmations to preach. Without them the young will not listen to me; for even the young grow tired of denials. The negative-monger falls before the soldiers, the men of action, the fighters, strong in the old, uncompromising affirmations which give them status, duties, certainty of consequences; so that the pugnacious spirit of man in them can reach out and strike deathblows, with steadfastly closed minds. Their way is straight and sure; but it is the way of death; and the preacher must preach the way of life. Oh, if I could only find it ! I am ignorant : I have lost my nerve and am intimidated : all I know is that I must find the way of life, for myself and all of us, or we shall surely perish.

(Act III)

To bring the foregoing up to date, one need only substitute Hell's Angels or the Black Septemberists or any other guerrilla groups for Shaw's 'soldiers' and once again the growing

---

[7] 'There must be a fusion between our religion and the rest of our culture, since there is no valid distinction between the laws of God and Nature, and Man must live by them no less than any other creature. Such a belief must be central to the philosophy of the stable society, and must permeate all our thinking.' *A Blueprint for Survival,* p. 22.

polarization of society, already remarked upon, is revealed; a polarization, moreover, which is increasingly evident and capable of diagnosis, but seemingly not susceptible to prescription.

Secondly, the past has a great deal to offer both in terms of beauty and as a necessary intellectual foil to the present. It is chastening to realize, for example, that the great landscape gardeners of the eighteenth century, men such as Kent, Brown and Repton, did not live to see their gardens, lakes and trees which they envisaged in their mind's eye come to full maturity. The gardens of Rousham House in Oxfordshire, for example, which Kent designed (and which is the only remaining unspoiled example of his work) must have taken at least a century to approach their full perfection, and clearly indicate that their eighteenth-century owner and planner shared alike a robust faith in the future and a sense of concern for generations then unborn. Moreover, there was no question of the modern ruthless attitude towards nature; on the contrary, as Pope (himself a keen amateur landscape-gardener) expressed it:

> To build, to plant, whatever you intend,
> To rear the column, or the arch to bend,
> To swell the terrace, or to sink the grot;
> *In all, let Nature never be forgot. . . .*
> Consult the genius of the place in all;
> That tells the waters or to rise, or fall;[8]

There is no lack of tree-planting, today, but almost all of it is directed towards a commercial and utilitarian end and is therefore confined to the fast-growing varieties, such as Norway and Sitka spruce, Douglas firs, European and Japanese larches; these are chiefly grown for the manufacture of paper and allied industries and although they do indicate an environmental concern, they nevertheless are yet another example of the short-term view and do not reveal the same faith in the future as does the planting of, say, an acorn.[9]

---

[8] *Epistle to Burlington*, 47–50; 57–58.
[9] The figures for the year ending March, 1972 relating to the planting of trees in Great Britain by the Forestry Commission are as follows: Conifers 21,632 hectares; broad-leaf (mainly oak and beech) 126 hectares! These figures do not, of course, take into account any private plantings.

No one in his right mind wants to return to the days when women who were unruly or licentious were ducked in the village pond, or when a malefactor whose only crime might have consisted of 'pocket-picking of more than 12d' or breaking a pane of glass after five p.m. 'with the purpose of stealing' was sentenced to be publicly hanged, but on the other hand many of the attitudes and views of the eighteenth century were in some ways more enlightened than our own. As Rattray Taylor has observed 'many people contrived to be happy and productive, free of stress and existential despair'.[10] It is an example of crass temporal provincialism to fasten on the ugly and vicious aspects of the century while ignoring the peace and serenity of the faces of the subjects painted by Reynolds and Gainsborough. I am well aware that the most of those who sat for these artists were aristocratic, but simply because certain good qualities were restricted in any given period to a small and privileged class does not render them less good. Rather one should seek to preserve and inculcate them in an ever-increasing number of people, particularly when such qualities are life-enhancing and sustaining, both of men and of nature, and of the vital inter-relationship which must exist between the two.

The neo-classicists of the first half of the eighteenth century were (as I have pointed out elsewhere) acutely aware of the thin partitions which separate man from brute. Swift's Yahoos were a terrible object lesson in what could happen to man if he were to reject reason and abandon himself exclusively to his passions. Poets, novelists, philosophers and theologians throughout this period attempted to impress upon society (or at least the cultivated, literate section of it) the need for restraint and control. Samuel Johnson, a man who spent his life-time combatting an excessively passionate and melancholic nature, expressed clearly and concisely the attitude of a large number of his contemporaries when he observed that 'whatever withdraws us from the power of our senses . . . advances us in the dignity of thinking beings.' In other words (to use the terminology of the late Pitirim Sorokin of Harvard) it was a deliberate attempt to supplant a 'sensate' culture with an 'ideational' one. It adhered to a somewhat strict and formalized code of behaviour which may repel many people today, yet F. R. Leavis has pointed out that

10 *Rethink*, p. 155.

this insistence on 'good form' was more than merely a social façade :

> With Dryden begins the period of English literature when form is associated with Good Form, and when, strange as it may seem to us, Good Form could be a serious preoccupation for the intelligent because it meant *not mere conformity* to a code of manners but a cultivated sensitiveness to the finest art and thought of the time. . . . Politeness was not merely superficial : it was the service of a culture and a civilization.[11]

Man saw himself as a being in harmony with the universe, which in turn was seen as the outward manifestation of the mind of the Creator. As Pope, again, expressed it :

> All are but parts of one stupendous whole,
> Whose body Nature is, and God the soul.[12]

The question which occupied the minds of thinking men and women was how man could best *attain* a state approaching the perfection of the universal order which he believed surrounded him. In other words, man actually strove to perfect *himself,* unconsciously anticipating Voltaire's dictum recommending the cultivation of one's own garden.

> Self-love but serves the virtuous mind to wake,
> As the small pebble stirs the peaceful lake;
> The centre moved, a circle straight succeeds;
> Another still, and still another spreads;
> Friend, parent, neighbour, first it will embrace;
> His country next, and next all human race.[13]

Such a striving was not so much, initially at least, an *external* one but one which involved a conscious effort towards self-betterment, the underlying belief being that if each man strove in this direction, society, composed of individual beings, would perceptibly improve as a result.

Contemporary attitudes are seemingly based upon an almost directly contrary view. For example, I have on my desk a mimeographed sheet, produced jointly by Marshall McLuhan and Marshall Fishwick, entitled 'Popular Culture Mosaic' in which under the sub-heading 'Art' the authors write :

---

[11] *Revaluation* (New York, 1963), pp. 76, 77.
[12] *Essays on Man,* I, 267–268.
[13] *Ibid,* IV, 363–368.

'Popular art *strives* to be *relaxing,* cathartic. High art says *stretch;* popular art says *relax.*'

Ignoring for the moment the oxymoron contortion of striving to relax, it must be apparent that if such art aims at inducing relaxation in its public, it has much in common with the mindless hedonism proclaimed in 'For My Son', and is further evidence of fatalism and a surrender to forces over which, or so we are induced to believe, we have no longer any control.

Of much greater significance is the contemporary tendency, already referred to in a previous chapter, for the natural idealism of youth to be harnessed to distant causes and abstractions, of which they can know little at first-hand and over which they can have even less control. The nations of the 'Third World' are a good example; the youthful can easily be induced to feel a wholly laudable and natural sympathy for the inhabitants of a country ten thousand miles away, ravaged by disease and poverty, illiteracy and starvation. With youthful impatience it then becomes a necessity to find an instant scapegoat for these intolerable conditions and unwilling (because untaught) to work through the logical thought-processes to account for the situation (such as poor methods of agriculture, insufficient or irregular rainfall, an endearing though unproductive indolence) they resort to a facile but comfortingly orthodox breed of Marxism and put the entire blame for a complex situation on 'capitalism'. This phenomenon, however idealistic in origin, betrays a sinister similarity to the attitude of German youth in the 'thirties, which was induced to believe that there was a *simple* origin of all the ills of the German people – Jewry; also that there was a *simple* solution to this problem – the extermination of the Jewish race. It says little for education that every generation seems destined, through ignorance of, or contempt for, the past, to perpetuate the miseries attendant upon a repudiation of cumulative wisdom.

As anyone who has read thus far will realize, this book is by no means uncritical of unbridled growth and capitalistic extortion. I am indeed deeply suspicious and critical of any attempt to measure human happiness or contentment exclusively in terms of welfare facilities or the number of telephones and refrigerators per thousand of the population, particularly as I have seen both in Britain and the United States a distinct decline in *happiness* since World War II, concurrent with a dramatically sharp increase in the material standard of living in these countries. To British readers who doubt the truth of this statement I would suggest that they visit a chromium-plated and neon-lit bar in central London, and watch the taut, nervous expressions on the customers' faces as they toy with spectacularly sophisticated drinks, and then visit an unspoiled village pub which still harbours a piano and a darts-board, and listen to the conversations and songs of the genuine villagers.

Perhaps the incessant harping on conditions in the under-developed nations springs from an unconscious and certainly unacknowledged desire to bring them kicking and struggling into the twentieth century, so that they too can enjoy the masochistic delights of high-rise living, trade-union bickerings, traffic-jams, urban neuroses and social alienation. Samuel Johnson cannot be dismissed as an intellectual light-weight or an unobservant student of human nature, and in *The Vanity of Human Wishes* (1749) he wrote :

> The needy traveller, serene and gay,
> Walks the wild heath, and sings his toil away.
> Does envy seize thee, crush the upbraiding joy,
> Increase his riches and his peace destroy.[14]

Whatever the motive, the tendency to focus on the plight of distant peoples and régimes, although undoubtedly connected with a growing global perspective, does vitiate and syphon off a great deal of energy and idealism from the more immediate and therefore much more complex domestic problems. Distance lends not only enchantment but also simplicity to the view and the questions posed by a proposed new urban clear-way are far more intricate and confusing and involve infinitely greater patience, understanding and logic than does, for example, a judgement on a distant authoritarian régime, which can be gratifyingly instant and passionate. Logically, moreover, it scarcely seems consistent to despise the fruits of materialism in one's own country while at the same time evincing a determination to raise the materialistic standards of living among the 'under-privileged' nations of the world. The idea of cultivating one's own garden may appear to be totally selfish and irresponsible, yet it must be the real solution to any and all human problems. A civilized society

---

[14] Lines 37–40.

can only exist if the *individual* members who comprise it are civilized in the best sense of that term. In other words, each human being should be educated so as to begin to mould his or her behaviour on principles which blend together compassion and logic. After all, there is little point in crying out to high heaven when one feels that materially one is being outwitted by a neighbour, if, the following day, one reverses the situation. This, then, is part of the task, and its implications and practical application may seem tedious and too slow. However, as Wynne-Tyson has pointed out in *The Civilised Alternative* :

> The destiny of mankind has never been decided by instant answers. All true growth is a painfully slow process, brought about not by over-night sensational purges, pogroms and liberations, but by the accumulated realizations and efforts of a significant minority of men and women who have developed their awareness to the point where they can grasp at least a grain of truth that mankind needs to see and accept wholly if we are to realize our potential.

Organizations, unfortunately, too often pander to people who are still stuck in the puerile morass of 'isms' and want to shelter cosily in the comfort of a polarized group. Frequently, too, they become ends in themselves, and the energies of their members become increasingly directed simply towards the preservation of the organization to the neglect of the real purpose for which it was formed. Organized Christianity, for example, bears little resemblance to the teachings of Christ, and similarly Communism in Russia (a country which, ironically, he hated) or its satellites would not be readily recognizable or accepted by Karl Marx as a practical application of his philosophy. Aware, possibly, of the fate that had overtaken his illustrious predecessors, Freud appears, towards the end of his life, to have become increasingly apprehensive of the length to which his future disciples would seek to extend and amplify his theories. There is the well-attested account of the remark he made in a lecture in Vienna towards the close of his career. Holding a cigar in his hand he declared : 'We all know what this is, but let us not forget that it is also a cigar and should be smoked.'

Thirdly, and lastly, contemporary ideas need to be weighed and contrasted not against others of the same period, but against those of the past, and it is here that the average modern student, regardless of his special field, is defenceless.

He is, as I think a large number of teachers would agree, rooted in what I have referred to as temporal provincialism, his interests and leisure reading confined, to a large extent, to contemporary film-makers, television pundits, writers and thinkers. The dangers implicit in this were admirably discussed and described by T. S. Eliot who, after questioning the validity of the belief that truth will eventually and effortlessly emerge from merely allowing a clash of contemporary ideas to take place, wrote as follows :

> If the mass of contemporary authors were really individual-
> ists, every one of them inspired Blakes, each with his
> separate vision, and if the mass of the contemporary public
> were really a mass of *individuals* there might be something
> to be said for this attitude. But this is not, and never has
> been and never will be . . . For the reader of contemporary
> literature is not, like the reader of the established great
> literature of all time, exposing himself to the influence
> of divers and contradictory personalities; he is exposing
> himself to a mass movement of writers, who, each of them,
> think that they have something individually to offer, but are
> really all working together in the same direction. And there
> never was a time, I believe, when the reading public was
> so large, or so hopelessly exposed to the influence of its own
> time.[15]

In the next chapter, the role of specialization as a contributory factor to the present malaise will be discussed.

---

[15] 'Religion and Literature', *Essays Ancient and Modern* (New York, 1936).

CHAPTER VIII

Contemporary Idols
of the Cave

———◆———

I soon learned what is undoubtedly the principal
reason for the paucity of published reports on skua
sightings since the first expeditions went into the
interior. Most of the scientists today are specialists
in some narrow technique, without broad cultivation
or the universal curiosity identified with the scientific
spirit as represented by Humboldt, by Darwin, and
by Wilson. At McMurdo, for example, lunching with
a scientist who had just come from an interior station
where he had been some weeks, I asked whether any
birds had been seen there. Yes, he replied, he had
himself seen birds there.

'What kind?' I asked.

'I don't know,' he said, 'I'm a physicist, not an
ornithologist.'

When I asked if he could tell me anything about
what the birds had looked like – their size, shape, or
colour – he answered that he hadn't noticed, again
adding that he was not an ornithologist but a
physicist.

(At a station in a dry valley of the interior, when I
asked one of the resident scientists the reason for a
spectacular peculiarity in the formation of the
glaciers all around us, he answered: 'I don't know,
I'm a meteorologist, not a glaciologist.' I was left to
wonder what kind of meteorologist it was who remained so uninterested in phenomena that were, after
all, the products of meteorological circumstances. But
the truth is that many of these scientists merely read
instruments or act as attendants on machines that
record on tape information that they don't have to
understand. Their data or the tapes are sent back
home for the knowledgeable to interpret.)

LOUIS J. HALLE, 'Eagle of the South Pole',
Audubon LXXV, No. 2 (March, 1973).

———◆———

The above is an excerpt from the author's book *The Sea and the Ice* and specifically treats of the skua, a close relative to the common gull. Although a shore bird, a great mystery resides in the fact that it has been sighted in the environs of the South Pole. It was curiosity arising from such sightings which prompted Halle's questioning of the unsuspecting and incurious 'scientists'. (McMurdo is the permanent scientific station-cum-staging point on Ross Island, which is on the edge of the great ice shelf and which serves as the point of entry for almost all polar expeditions. Readers may be pleased to know that in a subsequent paragraph Halle does acknowledge 'some . . . notable exceptions to this lack of intellectual curiosity', the most extensive and useful of which apparently emanated from the Soviet expeditions, based at Vostok, in the interior.)

What the passage does reveal, however, is the well-nigh suicidal specialization which currently passes for education in most countries, today.

Newman's concept of a university was that of an intellectual institution performing for the mind, the same function as a gymnasium does for the body – in other words to exercise the *whole* intellect. No healthy man in his right senses would attend a gymnasium daily for the sole purpose of exercising his right arm or his left leg to the absolute neglect of his other limbs. If such a physical programme were followed he would end up with one limb functioning perfectly while the others would be hopelessly withered and weak – in short, a crippled individual. Mentally, over-specialization has resulted in a similar crippling of our entire society – in a paradoxical, absurd civilization which has lost direction and meaning because the parts no longer function for the ultimate good of the whole. As a small but symbolic example one might cite the fact that Dr. Paul Ehrlich is stressing the absolute necessity for population control *now* while simultaneously organ-transplanters in various parts of the world are striving 'officiously to keep alive' ever-growing numbers. Should the latter succeed and produce a cheap and efficient method of transplanting human organs, the application of which could be widespread, one wonders if they would even then ponder the long-range effects of such on the unequal contest between population and food, population and space, population and human dignity.

In addition to the course in elementary (and not analytic)

logic which I have already suggested as a pre-requisite for all professions, could not courses be devised at universities and colleges to emphasis the historical and philosophical backgrounds of chemistry, physics and biology, and to subject some of the basic attitudes which many (though by no means all) specialists in these subjects appear to exhibit, to a vigorous, critical scrutiny in the context of environmental catastrophe? The fact that such an approach has been mooted and that random applications have been made is encouraging, but it is the four-year undergraduate curriculum at St John's College, Maryland (a small liberal arts college with a branch campus at Sant Fe, New Mexico) which would seem to serve as an example worthy of close inspection and possibly adoption elsewhere. This entire curriculum is devised as a corrective to specialization, and is an outgrowth of an idea extending back over a period of forty years, drawing on similar core curricula at Columbia College, the University of Chicago and the University of Virginia. The purpose is to give each undergraduate the opportunity to become acquainted with the intellectual history of western civilization (a period of nearly three thousand years), and aims 'to help the student to discover a new kind of historical perspective and perceive through all the historical shifts and changes the permanence and ever-present gravity of human issues.' Here is the most recent list of books which form the four-year degree course; it is subject to constant review and revision by a faculty committee :

FRESHMAN YEAR

Homer :	*Iliad, Odyssey*
Herodotus :	*History**
Aeschylus :	*Agamemnon, Choephoroe, Eumenides, Prometheus Bound*
Sophocles :	*Oedipus Rex, Oedipus at Colonus, Antigone*
Euripides :	*Hippolytus, Medea*
Aristophanes :	*Clouds, Birds*
Plato :	*Ion, Gorgias, Meno, Republic, Apology, Crito, Phaedo, Symposium, Parmenides,* Theaetetus, Sophist, Timaeus, Phaedrus*
Thucydides :	*The Peloponnesian War*
Aristotle :	*On the Soul,* Physics,* Metaphysics,* Nicomachean Ethics,* Politics,* Organon,* Poetics*

* Books read only in part

Euclid:	*Elements**
Lucretius:	*On the Nature of Things*
Lavoisier:	*Elements of Chemistry**
Nicomachus:	*Arithmetic**

SOPHOMORE YEAR

Epictetus:	*Discourses** *Manual*
Apollonius:	*Conics, I–III*
Virgil:	*Aeneid*
*The Bible**	
Tacitus:	*Annals**
Plutarch:	*Lives**
Gibbon:	*The Decline and Fall of the Roman Empire*
Ptolemy:	*Almagest**
Galen:	*On the Natural Faculties*
Plotinus:	*Fifth Ennead*
Augustine:	*Confessions*
Song of Roland	
Anselm:	*Proslogium*
Thomas Aquinas:	*Summa Theologica,** *Summa Contra Gentiles**
Dante:	*The Divine Comedy*
Chaucer:	*The Canterbury Tales**
Rabelais:	*Gargantua and Pantagruel**
Machiavelli:	*The Prince, Discourses**
Luther:	*A Treatise on Christian Liberty, Secular Author-ity*
Calvin:	*Institutes**
Copernicus:	*On the Revolution of the Spheres**
Montaigne:	*Essays**
Bacon:	*Novum Organum*
Kepler:	*Epitome of Copernican Astronomy, IV, V*
Donne:	Poems*
Shakespeare:	*Richard II, Henry IV,* Part I & Part II, *As You Like It, Twelfth Night, Othello, Hamlet, Macbeth, King Lear, The Tempest, Coriolanus*
Harvey:	*On the Motion of the Heart and Blood*
Darwin:	*The Origin of Species**

JUNIOR YEAR

Cervantes:	*Don Quixote*
Galileo:	*Two New Sciences**
Descartes:	*Rules for the Direction of the Mind,** *Discourse on Method, Geometry,** *Meditations*
Hobbes:	*Leviathan**
Spinoza:	*Theologic-Political Treatise*
Milton:	*Paradise Lost,** *Samson Agonistes*
Pascal:	*Pensées**

* Books read only in part

D

Racine:	*Phèdre*
Newton:	*Principia,* *Optics**
Huygens:	*Treatise on Light**
Locke:	*Essay Concerning Human Understanding,** *Second Treatise of Government*
Berkeley:	*Principles of Human Knowledge*
Leibniz:	*Discourse on Metaphysics, Monadology*
Swift:	*Gulliver's Travels*
Fielding:	*Tom Jones*
Hume:	*Enquiry Concerning Human Understanding, Dialogues Concerning Natural Religion*
Rousseau:	*The Social Contract*
Adam Smith:	*The Wealth of Nations**
Kant:	*Critique of Pure Reason,* *Critique of Practical Reason,* *Fundamental Principle of the Metaphysics of Morals*

Declaration of Independence, Articles of Confederation, United States Constitution

Madison, Jay:	*The Federalist**
Melville:	*Billy Budd, Benito Cereno*

SENIOR YEAR

La Fontaine:	*Fables**
Goethe:	*Faust**
Hegel:	*Philosophy of History,* *Preface to the Phenomenology of Spirit, Logic,* *Philosophy of Right**
Kierkegaard:	*Fear and Trembling, Philosophical Fragments*
Lobachevski:	*Theory of Parallels**
Marx:	*Capital,* *Communist Manifesto, Preface to Critique of Political Economy,* *Economic and Philosophic Manuscripts**
Tolstoi:	*War and Peace*
Nietzsche:	*Birth of Tragedy, Beyond Good and Evil*
Austen:	*Pride and Prejudice*
Dostoevski:	*The Possessed, Crime and Punishment, The Brothers Karamazov, The Idiot*
Baudelaire:	*Poems**
Wagner:	*Tristan and Isolde*
Freud:	*A General Introduction to Psychoanalysis*
Tocqueville:	*Democracy in America**

Documents from American Political History

Pierce:	*Philosophical Papers**
Valéry:	*Poems**
Einstein:	*On the Electrodynamics of Moving Bodies*

* Books read only in part

When this curriculum was first introduced at the college in 1937, fears were expressed that post-graduate schools would shun young people with such a general degree. These have since proved groundless and St. John's graduates are now sought after because of their breadth of vision and general culture. What the curriculum does offer, and in this it differs markedly from hybrids such as the usual 'inter-disciplinary studies', is a genuine demand on the intellect, and it is thus above and beyond the seemingly interminable wrangle over shallowness versus narrowness. The late Mark Van Doren, who was himself a guest lecturer at St. John's, wrote of the syllabus :

It makes inexorable demands which are the same for all. Nor are they impossible demands; they are indeed more practicable than any others, because more rewarding. It is assumed by those who avoid great books that such books are especially difficult. The contrary is true. Most of them were written for everybody, in 'a basic language about everything'. A classic is always fresh, vernacular, sensible and responsible. Even the mathematical and scientific classics were written in a tradition which made them intelligible; if we have lost contact with that tradition, the thing to do is to regain it – by mastering its classics – so that we may cease to be the gapers at abstraction which half of us now are . . . Education is honoured when it is hard, but it is honoured more when it is hard and good. The human mind naturally delights in exercise. Any student is to be envied who has passed this much through his mind, and any teacher who does so annually.[1]

If, as it seems, there is a vital need to construct a syllabus which would indicate the inter-relationship of all knowledge, so that students can grow up in a world which has meaning and significance for them individually and collectively, then the curriculum at St. John's might well serve as a blueprint. It might be objected that the books read and studied are parochial in that they exclude the great oriental writers and philosophers, but surely if one is going to reject one's *own* culture it is, or ought to be, essential that one knows precisely *what* one is rejecting and guard against being gulled into a modish fad.

I am not entirely convinced that philosophies which are

---

[1] *Liberal Education* (Boston, 1959), pp. 151–153.

derived from alien cultures and which are rooted in, and have evolved from, a way of life and of thought so different from those which have characterized western man, particularly since the Renaissance, can be abandoned and exorcised by readings however extensive in the *Koran* or the *Bhagavad Gita,* any more than one can transplant an exotic shrub from the tropics and expect it to thrive effortlessly in a totally different climate. Even in that great melting-pot, the United States, it only requires a year or two of residence to recognize peoples of Slavic, Germanic, Italian, Irish or British extraction. Although their accents and way of life are the result of having settled in Maine, Virginia, Kansas or California, yet they retain the distinctive characteristics of their country of origin despite possibly two or three centuries of 'americanization'.

There is, moreover, presumably no reason why students at St. John's, or any other college or university, may not pursue other fields of interest such as oriental studies in their spare time. One of the recent educational fallacies has been the presumption that a student only learns what he or she is formally taught or takes courses in, under instruction. Whatever the deficiencies of the Oxbridge system the adherence to an academic year in which approximately only twenty-four weeks are devoted to formal study and instruction indicates what a minor emphasis, relatively speaking, was placed in the past on lectures, tutorials and prescribed reading compared with wide-ranging private study and self-education.

Since there is widespread ignorance in both countries regarding the precise nature of their educational systems, a brief outline of British and American education might not be out of place here, and may indicate the respective strengths and weaknesses of both. There are, of course, exceptions to the following, but I am more concerned here with presenting a general picture. In Britain, after suitable preparation at secondary level, the pupil, at approximately sixteen years of age, takes an examination known as the 'Ordinary' level of the General Certificate of Education. This examination is designed for those in the top twenty-five per cent of ability, but frequently is taken by a number below this range (there is also a Certificate of Secondary Education designed for those of lower academic ability), and is externally administered and graded. The pupil may sit it, theoretically at least, in as many subjects as desired; these may range from Russian to Handicraft or from Botany to Ancient Greek, but will almost always include English language and literature, mathematics, a modern language and a science subject. A bright pupil would normally aspire to seven or eight 'O' level passes and this, so far as formal instruction is concerned, marks the end of his general studies.

Provided he does not leave school, he now proceeds towards the 'Advanced' level examination, which demands a further two years of formal study and instruction. This examination, which is also externally administered and graded, involves a degree of specialization and normally the pupil will have decided to take three, or at the most four, subjects. Although it is gradually becoming easier to take a mixture of both arts and science subjects, the tendency is still to specialize in one or the other. Thus at the age of eighteen in Britain a typical science student would obtain his 'A' levels in physics, chemistry and mathematics, while his 'arts' contemporary might have opted for, let us say, English, History and German. Upon the success or failure at 'A' level will depend his or her chances of gaining admission to a university, since in most subjects the numbers seeking a university place far exceed the vacancies. (American readers should bear in mind that there are only forty-two universities serving the entire population of England, Scotland and Wales – some fifty million people.[2])

Provided the pupil does sufficiently well in his 'A' levels, and obtains admission to a university, his three-year B.A. degree course will be even more specialized. It is theoretically possible for a British graduate in economics or chemistry never to have read Bacon or Milton, Freud or Jung; similarly one can obtain a degree in English or history with no knowledge of Newtonian physics or the quantum theory. For a British undergraduate 'reads' one subject only at university, although most subjects do require additional reading, usually involving a foreign language. In consequence the holder of a British B.A. degree after three years (each year consisting of three academic terms) has, in American equivalence and assuming

---

[2] This figure is somewhat misleading, since entry into many careers such as elementary-school teaching and nursing which require a B.A. degree in the USA are, in the United Kingdom, open to people holding diplomas and in the case of teachers these are granted by teacher-training colleges. The rapidly growing polytechnics are also empowered to grant degrees.

each American term or semester to carry approximately sixteen hours of 'credit', earned 144 hours in his 'major' or
specialized field. This is tantamount to the requirement for a
doctorate at an American university. The narrowness of the
British higher educational system has come under a certain
amount of attack in recent years, the most furious of which,
because it spotlighted in a dramatic fashion two well-known
and highly-respected protagonists, was the Snow–Leavis controversy of 1959 to 1962.

Because some fourteen years have elapsed since Sir Charles
(now Lord Snow) gave his celebrated, and as I have
already suggested, somewhat uneven lecture, 'The Two
Cultures and the Scientific Revolution', it is perhaps worth
recalling what he said on that occasion. After castigating
scientists (albeit rather mildly) for their ignorance of literature
and of traditional culture in general, as a result of which
'they are self-impoverished', Snow turned next to non-scientific
minds :

> They are impoverished too – perhaps more seriously, because
> they are vainer about it . . . They give a pitying chuckle
> at the news of scientists who have never read a major work
> of English literature. They dismiss them as ignorant special-
> ists. Yet their own ignorance and their own specialization
> is just as startling. A good many times I have been present
> at gatherings of people, who, by the standards of the
> traditional culture, are thought highly educated and who
> have with some considerable gusto been expressing their
> incredulity at the illiteracy of scientists. Once or twice I
> have been provoked and have asked the company how
> many of them could describe the Second Law of Thermo-
> dynamics. The response was cold : it was also negative.
> Yet I was asking something which is about the scientific
> equivalent of: *Have you read a work of Shakespeare's*?[3]

Some universities, notably Sussex and East Anglia, have in
recent years attempted to avoid the perils of specialization to
which Snow referred. In May 1973 a radical revision of the
'A' level syllabus was suggested by the influential Schools
Council, which, with Government and local authority back-
ing, works out school curricula and examinations. This
proposal envisions a two-year course leading to an examination

---

[3] *Cultures in Conflict: Perspectives on the Snow–Leavis Controversy*,
ed. Cornelius and St. Vincent (Chicago, 1964), p. 8.

at the age of eighteen in *five* subjects. All of these could be taken at normal ('N') level, while two or three could be attempted at further ('F') level. Although this proposal does afford a welcome relief from the rigorous specialization of sixth-form studies it is unlikely to be implemented until 1978–79 and it is to be hoped that in the interim some happier symbol than 'F' (with its unfortunate transatlantic connotation) can be suggested.

In the United States, superficially at least, a great deal of education (including the first two years at university) is devoted to general studies. There a child normally starts grade school at the age of six, and for the next twelve years (barring unusual circumstances) progresses through one grade per year. The system is more rigid than in Britain and head teachers or school principals enjoy less autonomy and choice in the selection of text-books or even in the selection of their own staff or 'faculty'. (So entrenched is the grade system that, more often than not, a child when asked his age will simply reply 'I'm in fifth grade' or 'eighth grade'.) Apart from such exceptions as the New York Regents' Examination, the pupil is graded or marked internally by his or her own teachers. At secondary level, grades in the various subjects studied are collated and arranged, forming very largely the credentials for subsequent admission to university or college. The latter, even when reinforced by external tests such as the College Entrance Examination Board, are invariably of the 'multiple-choice' variety, and essay-writing is a comparative rarity. Nor, apart from highly prestigious universities such as Harvard, Yale, Chicago, Columbia, Stanford and Princeton, or liberal arts colleges such as Amherst, Oberlin or Kenyon, do the same pressures regarding admission apply to the American potential undergraduate.

With some 2,500 institutions of 'higher learning' in the United States alone and with the constant growth and proliferation of junior colleges meeting the demands for the first two years of university work, any student who 'graduates' from high school with even a barely respectable grade-point average can gain entry into some university or college. At the state university at which I teach, for example, by law any pupil who graduates in the top seventy-five per cent from a high school within the state has to be admitted and thus, in the freshman and sophomore years at least, one has to recognize that potentially up to one third of the students attending the university may be *below* the median of *national intelligence.*

If one opens an American university catalogue, however, the whole splendour of a renaissance education seems available – Agriculture and Forestry, Agronomy, Animal Nutrition, Astronomy, Bacteriology, Biology, Business Marketing, Chemistry, Drama, English, Foreign Languages (including French, German, Greek, Italian, Latin, Russian, Spanish and Swahili), Forest Engineering, Geology, Geography, History, Human Management and Family Economics, Industrial Arts, Journalism, Landscape Architecture, Law, Library Science, Mathematics, Mining, Music, Philosophy, Physics, Physical Education and Safety, Political Science, Psychology, Social Work, Special Education, Speech Communication, Statistics and Computer Science – until one arrives rather breathlessly at Zoology.[4] Here surely is an intellectual diet to whet even the most jaded of sophomore palates, and certainly after four years spent in studying such subjects one should be liberally educated.

Unfortunately, the very system militates against a truly liberal education. Obtaining a B.A. degree in the United States is not only a longer, but an infinitely more complicated process than it is in the United Kingdom, involving required courses, class attendance and a constant barrage of 'quizzes' and other examination hurdles more associated in British minds with a school than a university. The academic year traditionally is divided into two semesters, each one lasting approximately fifteen weeks. (Certain universities and colleges have now adopted the trimester or 'quarter' system, but this in no material way affects the observations which follow.) An incoming freshman will normally 'register' for five courses, each one earning three 'credit hours'. This means that each week he will spend three hours in class in each of the five subjects he has elected; thus he will be in class for a total of fifteen hours each week, and such classes are usually a mixture of formal lecture and informal discussion, the tutorial system being virtually unknown. If one adds to this an additional thirty hours for written assignments and preparations (together with the fact that a large percentage of American

---

[4] All the above, with many course offerings omitted, have been taken from a current catalogue of an average-sized mid-Western State University.

undergraduates have part-time jobs either in the university or city to help them pay their own way to the degree) then clearly, mentally and physically, they are unable to indulge, to any real extent, their own intellectual interests, to explore some idea or concept exhaustively in the library, or even to assimiliate the knowledge which is being relentlessly thrust at them. This process continues throughout the first two years of an undergraduate career, during which the student is largely occupied in getting various 'requirements' out of the way in order to prepare for his 'major' or special field of interest. Thus someone whose eventual aim is to secure his degree in English history will nevertheless be obliged to take a course, or courses in philosophy, psychology, a science subject and a foreign language, and maintain at least a 'C' average in all these, before he can begin to specialize. Even in his third or fourth year he will still carry a 'class-load' (and the term is both revealing and expressive) of between fifteen and, exceptionally, twenty-one class hours per week. When he has accumulated sufficient hours (the average is around 130), and providing his grade-point average is a 'C' or above, he receives his B.A. degree.

From my own personal knowledge it is not only possible, but frequently happens, that a semi-literate can gain admission to a large state university, and, because the sheer size of the classes he attends precludes any examinations requiring essay-writing, coast along through objective tests and quizzes (the material for which can be learnt by rote) and emerge, still semi-literate, after four years with a B.A. degree in some fairly undemanding discipline. Frequently, too, students complain that they may take an entire course, lasting fifteen or sixteen weeks, and never actually see the 'results' of any test they have taken – merely a numerical score on a computer sheet. Consequently, it is difficult for them to ascertain what errors they may have committed, and they are precluded from even the remotest hope of being able to remedy such errors. Under these circumstances the devaluation of the first degree has reached astonishing proportions, and the same lowering of status has inexorably overtaken the master's degree (preparation for which is similarly based on class-attendance and credit-hours), leaving the Ph.D. to survive as the only really respectable academic qualification. Let me re-emphasize that the foregoing is emphatically *not* an accurate picture of the Ivy-league colleges or others of the same class, but it does

D*

present an undistorted and unprejudiced description of the majority of the eight million young Americans currently attending institutions of higher learning; many of these young people have no aptitude or inclination for mental application and are bereft of any real intellectual curiosity, but parental and societal pressures have combined to persuade them that a 'degree-less life is not worth living'. In consequence trade and craftsmanship have become increasingly rare, sought-after and amply rewarded; my wife for many years has preserved, in the kitchen of our house in the United States a little piece of graffiti which bears the legend : 'Cheer up ! Your plumber is naming his new yatch after you.'

What is particularly frustrating to the good student (and every year at every one of the 2,500 colleges and universities in the United States there are many) is that, because of the vast number of courses offered during any given semester and the consequent mammoth task of scheduling each one, it is virtually impossible for an interested student to take complementary courses simultaneously. For example, it would be beneficial and indeed highly desirable to both teacher and taught, if a student taking a course in eighteenth-century literature could at the same time be taking courses in eighteenth-century British history, philosophy, art and music, so that the writings of the period could be seen in their *complete* setting and the essential ethos of the period captured. In practice, however, more often than not, the literature course may be taken in the second year and the history or philosophy courses deferred until the third or even the fourth year. The result is a fragmentary education designed, it would almost seem, to prohibit any possibility of students being able to take Newman's 'connected view'; the final result is again 'acquisition' and not 'philosophy'. Such an education has been described by the American scholar, R. F. Baum, as 'a cultural bazaar wherein, guided by nothing more than his own usually haphazard inclinations and information, the student samples wholly unconnected and often trivial fragments of man's knowledge.'[5]

Eventually, of course, in a pyramidal fashion, the American post-graduate does specialize and the master's and doctoral programmes are directed at achieving the same narrow results

---

[5] 'A Mediaeval Institution in Crisis', *The Intercollegiate Review*, Spring 1973, p. 185.

as in Britain only at a somewhat later stage; there is in the United States, too, a small but growing feeling that this trend can spawn dangers not only academically, but also culturally and environmentally. A respected philosopher. Dr. Howard Slaatte, in a forthcoming book, *Modern Science and the Human Situation,* expresses himself as follows :

> Facts and more facts do not guarantee insight and under-standing; techniques are no substitute for content; knowl-edge cannot be divorced from values . . . Educators must come to see afresh that specialization can spell a new barbarism unless conjoined with cultural values. Merely passing on information as a set of recipes belongs not in a university but in a school for technicians.

The St. John's College brochure expresses it rather more succinctly : 'The Ph.D. degree is not a barrier to appointment [at the college], but teachers here are expected to rise above it.'

On neither side of the Atlantic (with the exception of isolated programmes such as St. John's) is there any real attempt to convey the richness and diversity of our common cultural heritage, and in the light of prevailing conditions it is small wonder that the counter-culture or sub-culture had such an easy task in its initial encroachment and subse-quent take-over of college campuses throughout the western world. For it provided, apart from glamorous figures with whom the disenchanted young could identify and the oppor-tunity of repudiating adult attitudes and *mores,* a simplistic but *homogeneous* message of 'liberty' and unbridled licence. It may have originated in Liverpool, but its message was most avidly and uncritically accepted in the United States, in which country the educational system virtually precludes the *historical* background necessary to appreciate for example the full disillusionment with the licentiousness of 'liberty' which a writer such as Milton experienced, and which he expressed so eloquently in the sonnet of which the opening line reads 'I did but prompt the age to quit their clogs,' and which ends :

> Licence they mean when they cry Liberty;
> For who loves that [liberty] *must first be wise and good;*
> But from that mark how far they move we see
> For all this waste of wealth and loss of blood.
> [My italics]

(Curiously enough, Shelley at the age of twenty-six reached

much the same conclusion. In his *Preface* to *Prometheus Unbound*, composed largely in the ruined Baths of Caracalla in 1818-19, he wrote : '*until the mind can love, and admire, and trust and hope and endure,* reasoned principles of moral conduct are seeds cast upon the highway of life which the unconscious passsenger tramples into dust . . .')

Returning, however, to specialization, it is one of the tragic ironies of our age that just at the moment when the problems of the environment are seen to be inextricably *related*, university specialists and indeed specialists in all walks of life are becoming more specialized. Since this chapter was begun, a week ago, two scientists at the Baylor College of Medicine at Waco, Texas announced at the annual meeting of American Experimental Biologists, the discovery that memory can be transferred from one rat to another. They stated that after a series of experiments, they had discovered that in rats' brains the memory of the sound of an electric bell is lodged in an eight-segment chain of six specific amino acids. These can apparently be isolated and subsequently injected into other untrained rats who thereafter behave *as if they have been trained.* (The news of this experiment received little notice in the press.) No doubt the response to this discovery by the other specialists at the meeting was one of suitable awe and admiration for a new 'breakthrough' in experimental biology and another triumph for mankind in its contest to ascertain the specific functions of the multitudinous cells which make up the brain.

The two scientists involved might have been asked the following, no doubt simplistic, questions.

1) Why did you perform the experiment? Were you impelled by curiosity, a desire for professional recognition, a concern for knowledge for its own sake, financial reward, a combination of all these, or some other less obvious motive?[6]

2) Since the experiment could conceivably be extended and

---

[6] In all fairness one must admit, of course, that this question is equally applicable to all fields of human endeavour from the attempt to climb Mount Everest to the writing of this particular book. The layman, however, continues to be 'blinded by science'. One constantly comes across naïve beliefs such as the automatic assumption that, because a researcher is engaged in the task of finding a cure for cancer, he must be terribly concerned for his fellow-men. This is roughly analogous to assuming that Hillary and Tensing climbed Everest because they wanted to see the view from the top. It is not the

expanded to human brains and human memory, did you consider carefully all the possible implications not just of the
experiment itself, but of the *wisdom* of *imparting* the result
of your findings to the world in a century which has recently
witnessed other interesting experiments, this time on human
subjects, in Auschwitz, Buchenwald and other camps throughout Europe and Asia?

3) What benefits, both long- and short-term, do you think the
the publication of your research will provide? Please be as specific as possible. If the answer to this question is of an amelior-
istic nature, has the thought occurred to you that Leonardo da
Vinci suppressed his invention of the submarine because he
deemed it 'too devilish a contraption' to be placed in the
hands of fallible and possibly morally incompetent men?

4) Have you read any, or all of the following: Swift's
Gulliver's Travels, Book III (specifically the passages relating
to the Academy at Lagado); Taylor's *The Biological Time
Bomb* or *Rethink*; Huxley's *Brave New World* or Orwell's
1984? If you have read either of the last two, do you think
that the results of your research have deferred or hastened
the advent of the type of society which both authors envisaged? If in your opinion you have deferred it, please give
reasons; if, on the contrary, you have, in however small a
degree, hastened it, do you welcome such a society? If you do,
could you please inform those of us who dread it (or are
simply apprehensive of it) where we might go to avoid becoming enslaved by it?

5) Could you please be explicit about the sources of the
funds which enabled you to instigate and pursue the research?
What percentage of such, however indirectly, was obtained
from the tax-payer?

Perhaps some readers will regard some, or all, of these

---

result, but the challenge, that motivates all men and if we exclude the
scientist from such 'human' motives then we are abdicating our
responsibility of using our critical faculties. Dr James B. Conant,
former President of Harvard University, in *Modern Science and
Modern Man* wrote as follows on this same topic: 'The notion that
a scientist is a cool, impartial, detached individual is, of course,
absurd. The vehemence of conviction, the pride of authorship is borne
as fiercely among scientists as among any creative workers. Indeed, if
they did not, there would be no advance in science. But this emotional
attachment to one's own point of view is particularly insidious in
science because it is so easy for a proponent of a project to clothe
his convictions in technical language.'

questions as impertinent and unfair, but since my life, my children's lives and the lives of almost everyone living in an over-developed country are being changed, and in many instances dislocated and uprooted, by the application of such experiments, it is only just that those initially responsible for the consequences be held accountable.[7] The plea that scientific experimentation is neutral is today naïve; with the time-span between experimentation and application rapidly shrinking, the aristocratic ideal of 'pure' science referred to by Lynn White is definitely a phenomenon of the past. In *Future Shock,* Toffler observes that 2,000 years elapsed between the discovery of conic sections by Appollonius of Perga and the application of this discovery to engineering problems. A century elapsed between the invention of a machine in 1836 that 'mowed, threshed, tied straw into sheaves and poured grain into sacks' and its widespread adoption and marketing in the 1930s. Toffler, after giving other examples, including that of the typewriter (the first English patent for which was issued in 1714) and Appert's discovery of a method to can food, proceeds as follows :

> Today such delays between idea and application are almost unthinkable. It is not that we are more eager or less lazy than our ancestors, but we have, with the passage of time, invented all sorts of social devices to hasten the process. Thus . . . since the beginning of this century more than sixty per cent has been slashed from the average time needed for a major scientific discovery to be translated into a useful technological form. . . . The stepped-up pace of invention, exploitation and diffusion, in turn, accelerates the whole cycle still further. For new machines or techniques are not merely a product, but a source, of fresh creative ideas.[8]

As I have suggested elsewhere, as a civilization we have become so much better at *doing* things than understanding the *consequences* of our actions, for an understanding of the contemporary scene demands a certain amount of leisure and quietude for reflection, but it is precisely these conditions

---

[7] A 'Council for Science and Society' was launched in the United Kingdom in July 1973, under the Chairmanship of Sir Michael Swann, Vice-Chancellor of Edinburgh University and Chairman of the BBC. The main objective of the Council is to forewarn the Government and public of possible dangers before new products of science are put into mass misuse.

[8] *Future Shock,* pp. 27, 28.

which are significantly lacking in today's world – a world characterized by increased tempo and diminished rhythm. 'Leisure', wrote Shaw, 'is the sphere of individual liberty; labour is the sphere of slavery.'

One might expect those employed at universities to have time for reflection but, certainly as regards American universities, this is far from being the case. Apart from lecturing and teaching anything up to fifteen hours a week (together with continual reading and preparation for such) one is expected to sit on endless problem-shelving committees, to attend over-crowded academic conventions, to grade essays submitted by one's students (and these may amount to anything up to fifty reasonably lengthy ones per week), not to mention attempting to keep abreast of the latest research taking place in one's own discipline. The sabbatical leave originally intended as a period of intellectual refreshment has now declined in real value as its recipients tend to regard it as an opportunity for earning yet further degrees, or producing yet another promotion-earning piece of 'research'.

The establishment of 'think-tanks' is a logical and necessary response to such conditions, and providing their findings are heeded both by governments and populace at large and that those employed at them resist the twin evils of a rarified atmosphere on the one hand and demands for instant, short-term solutions on the other, their value to society may infinitely surpass their comparatively trifling cost. Above all, they should guard against and reject demands for 'relevance' (which as I have pointed out earlier is really topicality) which lead to piecemeal poulticing while ignoring the real causes of the disease. In this respect, they might do well to ponder the fate which has overtaken a number of well-known North American universities. Referring to these, Jacques Barzun, formerly Provost of Columbia University, has written as follows :

As a consequence of the Second World War the American government became aware that in the universities there were teachers who knew many *useful* things even outside the scientific realm. Academic men became known and earned respect from the public, so much so that they began to be in demand for peace-time activities. Thus was precipitated the movement known as the 'cult of research'. Not only did the public, industry, state and federal governments call upon the personnel of the universities for expert advice, but *insiders* generated the notion that research results were a universal obligation : one must 'produce'. In order to justify this new public respect and to satisfy this new public demand, social science, medicine, physics . . . became front-line exhibitions of what the university could *do*. The term used to describe the effort was 'public service'. Universities exchanged old 'education' for new public service and tacitly down-graded the teaching of the young.[9]

Government expectations eventually led to demands by students and faculties alike for special service : 'Both wanted the university to provide the full life. *Everything* should be supplied – entertainment, sociability, medical and psychiatric help, insurance and so on.'[10]

There is, today, an accelerating tendency for both universities and churches to concentrate on 'social work' and to divest themselves of their historic and, in my opinion, essential rôles. In the case of the former, this was primarily the education (in the best sense) of the young; in the latter, a concern for the *spiritual* life of man. A petrol station (and the comparison is in no way intended disrespectfully to any of the institutions) is vital to a motorist, but he must know precisely where it is. If it should suddenly don wheels and career off, mingling with the traffic, its essential function would be lost and it would simply further aggravate the problem of street congestion, leaving motorists stranded and bewildered. Possibly there are not enough secular agencies in existence to care for the poor, the destitute, the sick and lonely but if, as one suspects, there are now so many that they are duplicating each other's work, then perhaps it would be to the advantage of both universities and churches to resume their primary functions. Nor should it be a matter of concern if this results in a temporary drop in enrolment or membership. There must be many university teachers who would rather be at a college of two hundred students than at a 'multiversity' of fifty thousand the majority of whom consist of mere *trainees* (St. John's College attracts over 500 applicants for every teaching vacancy). At the former, too, the genuine student would feel less isolated and consequently, perhaps, display less arrogance and disdain, than do the small minorities of 'intellectuals' on

[9] 'The Decline of University Independence', *Education: Threatened Standards,* London, 1972, p. 93.
[10] *Ibid,* p. 96.

the mammoth campuses of North America. In the case of churches, a positive mania for innovation and change (ranging from the abandonment of the rich, poetic language of the King James Version to the allocation of funds for 'freedom-fighters' in Africa) has alienated many of the faithful while in no way attracting either the attendance or allegiance of the faith-less.[11]

Change has always been a facet of human experience and without it no progress is possible, but the rate of it, in the contemporary world, is, or ought to be, a matter for profound concern. *New* highways, *new* methods of transportation, *new* neighbourhoods, *new* schools, *new* supermarkets, *new* methods of food-preparation, *new* towns, *new* universities, *new* and daring sexual attitudes (although how we were all conceived in the past must be an overwhelming mystery to anyone under twenty-one), *new* packaging and distribution methods, *new* and often bizarre religions. The list is endless and Toffler concedes that 'future shock' is no longer a distantly potential danger, but a real sickness from which increasingly large numbers already suffer. This psycho-biological condition can be described in medical and psychiatric terms. It is the disease of *change*. Later in the book he writes :

> It is quite clearly impossible to accelerate the rate of change in society, or to raise the novelty ratio in society, without triggering significant changes in the body chemistry of the population. By stepping up the pace of scientific technology and social change, we are tampering with the chemistry and biological stability of the human race.[21]

In the light of this statement one may be pardoned for being astounded at his stated objective in writing *Future Shock* – 'to help us come to terms with the future . . . Towards this end, it puts forward a broad new theory of adaptation.' The determinism implicit in such an objective is too obvious to need emphasizing, but if we are ever to achieve a society characterized by order and harmony, a return to the Tennysonian ideal – 'all things in order stored' (predictably scorned and repudiated by Toffler) – then as a start to reinstituting a saner, less frenetic society those in

---

[11] W. H. Auden recently caused a minor furore by refusing to read the lesson at a church service in Yorkshire because the vicar insisted that the poet should read from the New English Bible.
[12] *Future Shock*, pp. 341, 342.

education should realize firstly that a deterministic attitude which forces us to become passive spectators of our global destiny is fallacious. Let me repeat that educators teach the *basic* skills on which all of Faustian men's progress depends; an illiterate society, lacking also numeracy, could not but regress. Unthinking, uncontrolled regression, however, would prove as calamitous as unthinking, uncontrolled growth and progress. Thus there is an urgent need for a system of values to be incorporated into our educational system from primary to university levels, for knowledge bereft of values is, as I have suggested earlier, the path to 'clever devilry'. Secondly, universities should set an example by clearly defining the limits to their function and goals and resist the Protean path to diversification and hyper-specialization.

University specialization, unfortunately, sounds so innocuous and is taken so much for granted that to challenge it may smack of philistinism, and even leave one open to the charge of being a Luddite. Without wishing to resemble Lévi-Strauss I should, nevertheless, like to suggest that there is at least a symbolic relationship between specialization and sectionalism, both of which tend to be characterized by blinkered vision. The perils of the former may, to the average reader, seem remote and academic; those of the latter are ever-present and have a direct application to our daily lives. As an example, Congress recently passed a $20 billion highway-construction bill but refused to allow any of this stupendous sum to be utilized for mass-transit systems, depite the fact that (as anyone who has visited or lived in the United States will realize) there has existed for years an urgent need for subsidies to the various public-transport authorities – a need which has been emphasized by a threatened petrol shortage this year and by the failure or obstruction of the production of a 'clean' car within the period called for by the administration. The question that must arise is, why did Congress act in a manner so directly contrary to advice from environmental experts, and indeed to basic common-sense? (The account in the press described the passage of this vast bill as being performed by a barely audible 'voice vote', with many members 'already racing towards *airports* to begin a ten-day Easter recess!') The answer is a dismal one and indicates how very far removed we are from a genuine sense of stewardship, or indeed from a truly responsible society. Members from the cities voted for the bill because it was in *their* interest to do so; those from rural areas voted against it because, presumably, they deemed it against *their* interest to give it support.[13] Yet let me repeat, all those voting had received an education, the majority possessing college degrees. Can one in all honesty be satisfied with an educational system which appears to produce men and women who have every grace except, apparently, an interest in creating a tolerable environment for themselves and their children to inherit.[14]

This plea for totality of vision may seem diametrically opposed to the concept of cultivating one's own garden which I extolled in the previous chapter, but if one looks closely at the quoted passage from the *Essay on Man*, it becomes apparent that Pope envisioned the 'man of sense' perceiving that an *isolated* 'garden' cannot exist either in nature or society. 'Self-love' may be a constant of human nature and one must, therefore, start by acknowledging its existence; once acknowledged, however, one can proceed, through the exercise of one's feelings and intellect, properly *blended and educated*, to the almost imperceptible but inexorable realization :

> That Reason, Passion, answer one great aim;
> That *true* Self-Love and Social are the same.

It is worth stressing that in these lines, Pope does not suggest that 'reason' divorced from 'passion' is enough. Reason alone can be hard, unimaginative and selfish; unalloyed

---

[13] 'The power requirements of transporting freight by road are five to six times greater than by rail, and the pollution is correspondingly higher. The energy outlay for the cement and steel required to build a motorway is three to four times greater than that required to build a railway, and the land area necessary for the former is estimated to be four times more than for the latter.' (*A Blueprint For Survival*). The authors of the same publication also make the following extremely pertinent observation: 'If we plan remedial action with our eyes on political rather than ecological reality, then very reasonably, very practicably, and very surely, we will muddle our way to extinction.'

[14] Stewart Udall, former Secretary of the Interior, writes as follows in *1976: Agenda For Tomorrow* (New York, 1972, p. 147): 'The Congress . . . has been the least adaptable, least dynamic entity of our constitutional triad. Only when its committees and individual members think and speak for the nation as a whole – and not as standput defenders of special interests or the narrow aims of the several states – is the Congress worthy of its highest mission.'

passion and emotionalism can be sentimental, cloying and egotistical. The fusion of the two was the *beau idéal* of the best minds of the early eighteenth century, with sentimentality (as opposed to sentiment) waiting in the wings, to emerge from 1750 onwards as the dominant mood both in literary and social terms.[15]

Let me attempt to translate the foregoing in a manner which the modern mind will have no difficulty in accepting as relevant. Imagine an old-fashioned 'iron-master', his views still deeply-rooted in laissez-faire economics. His reason tells him that he is making a handsome profit annually and with a house, fifteen or twenty miles from his factory's pollution or effluence, in a pleasant situation, why should he concern himself with the damage he may be doing to other people's lives and environment? Possibly, however, he may have grandchildren of whom he is extremely fond and whose future lies near to his heart. If with this emotional attachment, he also uses his reason, it must quickly become apparent to him that all rivers and streams are eventually one; that all generations are interdependent, and that there is *no* hiding-place from eco-catastrophe.

Until such a state of mind is widespread, however, one must reluctantly concede that mobility, whatever its cultural and recreational advantages, has temporarily created the delusion that one can separate one's private lives from the effects of one's work. If a law were passed tomorrow compelling *all* citizens of *all* over-developed countries to live within, let us say, four miles of their employment, one would witness within a year or two a greater measure of overall concern for our cities, towns and countryside than could be effected in half a century by all the environmental agencies in existence.

The crucial question inherent in all the foregoing must, however, be: Is man worth saving? If he is as destructive as ecologists say, then would not his disappearance from the natural scene be positively beneficial? In other words, no truly valid discussion of the hypothetical future of man can, in the last analysis, ignore the question of human value. If man is merely a 'naked ape' or 'a walking bag of sea-water'

---

[15] Henry MacKenzie's *The Man Of Feeling* (1771) and Goethe's *The Sorrows of Young Werther* (1774) are, in their different ways, good examples of this trend.

as certain scientists choose to regard him (and also, if they are logical, presumably themselves), or a complex but predictable collection of reactions to various stimuli as the behaviourists assert, then apart from a natural but sentimental loyalty to one's own kind, his disappearance from the scene would be merely another example of an expendable species, incapable of the necessary natural adaptations, 'cast as rubbish to the void'. Tennyson, despite certain other limitations, captured so well the full implications of this question when he wrote:

> And he, shall he,
> Man her last work, who seemed so fair,
> Such splendid purpose in his eyes,
> Who roll'd the psalm to wintry skies
> Who built him fanes of fruitless prayer . . .
>
> Who loved, who suffer'd countless ills,
> Who battled for the True, the Just,
> Be blown about the desert dust,
> Or seal'd within the iron hills?
> (*In Memoriam* LVI, 8–12; 17–20.)

As I have tried to indicate thus far, the question is no longer academic, but is of pressing importance and in the final chapter an attempt, however inadequate, will be made to justify the ways, not of God but of man, to contemporary men whose faith not just in a Creator, but also in themselves, appears spiritually and culturally to be waning.

CHAPTER IX

Is Man Worth Saving?

———————◆———————

He [man] is a fantastic thing that has developed
sensibilities and established values beyond the nature
which gave him birth. He is of all living creatures
the one to whom the earth is the least satisfactory.
He has arrived at a point where he can no longer
delude himself as to the extent of his predicament,
and should he either become modified or disappear
the earth would continue to spin and the grass to
grow as it has always done. Of the thousands of
living species the vast majority would be as unaware
of his passing as they are now unaware of his presence, and he would go as a shadow goes. His arts,
his religions, and his civilizations – these are fair and
wonderful things, but *they are fair and wonderful to
him alone.* With the extinction of his poetry would
come also the extinction of the only sensibility for
which it has any meaning, and there would remain
nothing capable of feeling a loss. Nothing would be
left to label the memory of his discontent 'divine',
and those creatures who find in nature no lack would
resume their undisputed possession of the earth.

    JOSEPH WOOD KRUTCH: *The Modern Temper* (1956,
my italics)

———————◆———————

In his penetrating analysis of the spiritual and cultural
malaise afflicting modern man, Krutch acknowledges that
such a malaise is not universal. Certain types of higher
intellect, epitomized by those of a particular scientific bent,
appear to find the laboratory and its contents all-sufficient.[1] At
the other end of the scale, in the case of property-developers

---

[1] 'For the American business careerist, success is a residual religious
vocation. It is *the* meaning, not *a* meaning, of life – and he cannot
tolerate suggestions that there may be highly divergent patterns of life
within which people find significance in ways totally different from
his.' *The Secular City,* p. 69.

and other business tycoons, the accumulations of wealth and power seems to satisfy all needs and no lack is perceived.

For most thinking, non-scientific minds, however, there does exist a profound feeling that there is an inconsistency between the world one wishes to inhabit and the material world revealed by science, and this has nothing to do with the imperfections, real or imaginary, of political and social systems. I 'know' that the desk at which I am writing these words is not 'solid' but consists of a myriad of particles involved in a ceaseless and apparently meaningless dance; that the room in which these words are being written, together with the house and the garden outside and the flowers 'smiling' in the sunshine are being whirled at vast speeds around the sun; that the universe, of which this entire world is a small and insignificant part, is itself tucked away in a remote part of the cosmos. The seventeenth-century English village in which I have spent the happiest days of my life was, in cosmic time, born a billionth of a second ago and is inevitably doomed to decay and death, in a similarly infinitestimal fraction of a 'moment'. Versailles and Blenheim, Venice, Rome and London, the 'lawns' of Entebbe and the 'grounds' at Charlottesville, even Burgon's 'rose-red city – half as old as Time' – all of these, so fair and so dear to many human hearts and on which much care and attention is (or has been) lavished, are transient and tragically ephemeral. This is what science teaches, and its message seems clear and unequivocal. In the presence of such evidence what room is there for ordinary human hopes and aspirations? What answer to these cold facts do the 'freedom' fighters and politicians of the world offer, and whence do they derive their panaceas?

This is apparently the *logically* and *empirically* proven condition of man and his world, and this scientific view has permeated and secularized (in the broadest and most expansive sense) a great deal of contemporary thought and literature. It is responsible for the shift from what I. A. Richards styled the 'Magical View' of the world to the strictly scientific, and although we still use terms such as 'sunrise' and 'sunset', avoid perhaps walking under ladders and spilling salt, we do so almost nostalgically, for if the sun *rises,* this world, our only habitat and the scene of all that is dear and familiar to us, is restored to what we feel to be its rightful place of prominence. Even the possibility of ill-luck brought about by smashing a mirror or spilling some salt, suggests, comfortingly, that man is not alone in the desolation of space and that there exists a supernatural and superior force ('fate' or 'the fates'), which betrays an active interest in human life and human actions. In our enlightened time, however, such beliefs are becoming increasingly rare and if we do speak of 'sunrise' we do so as a matter of habit, almost certainly unreflectingly, and if we cast a little spilled salt over our left shoulder (where the devil is supposedly lurking), we do so self-consciously and refer to such acts as 'superstitions', that is to say fears founded on *irrational* feelings or beliefs.

It is somehow appropriate that Aldous Huxley (the grandson of T. H. Huxley, the great Victorian scientist and materialist, who displayed such a robust and characteristic faith in the power of Truth and Knowledge to free mankind from the trammels of superstition) should write as follows in *Point Counter-Point* :

> The shaking air rattled Lord Edward's *membrana tympani*; the interlocked *malleus, incus,* and stirrup bones were set in motion so as to agitate the membrane of the oval window and raise an infinitesimal storm in the fluid of the labyrinth. The hairy endings of the auditory nerve shuddered like weeds in a rough sea; a vast number of obscure miracles were performed in the brain, and Lord Edward ecstatically whispered 'Bach!'[2]

From a strictly scientific view this is an accurate physiological account of what happens when one hears and responds to music, but no composer could be appreciated if the auditor were to be constantly aware of this process or to remind himself that his enjoyment of the music, rationally analyzed, consisted exclusively of memory of the last note and anticipation of the next.

One crucial question arising from the foregoing must be : Can man live with the knowledge of *total* truth about everything? This question may seem perverse and ludicrously academic until one realises that much of contemporary culture revolves around, and has its origin in, the idea of an 'absurd' universe, devoid of any ultimate meaning or significance, other than that which man himself fleetingly imparts to it. The so called 'Theatre of the Absurd' is one manifestation of such a view, and starting with the per-

[2] New York, 1928, p. 38.

formance of Alfred Jarry's play *Ubu Roi,* in Paris in 1896, the view of an absurd and therefore totally amoral universe has gained strength through a succession of plays and novels conveying the consequential absurdity of human life, hopes and dreams. Commenting upon Jarry's works, George Wellwarth (in *The Theatre of Protest and Paradox*) equates Ubu with the 'cosmic malignant force that pervades the *avant-garde* drama', and adds that when Jarry wrote the play 'he was rebelling not only against the outmoded conventions of the current drama . . . but against absolutely everything, including the world and the cosmos.'[3] Such a reaction would have puzzled Thomas Huxley who, in his day, somewhat naïvely believed that the structure of Christian morality would survive despite the fact that the supernatural props on which it was based had been first eroded and then removed. However, as Krutch succinctly and wryly observes :

> Westermarck, having adopted the genetic methods consecrated by Darwin and having armed himself with the detachment of science, plunges into the study of morals. We eagerly await the exact and positive conclusions which science seems to promise, and he returns with three fat volumes which prove – that morality does not exist.[4]

Huxley's contemporary and sometime antagonist, Matthew Arnold, apppears to have realized far more fully the prophetic nature of Dmitry Karamazov's anguished remark – 'How can man be good without God?' – and attempted to substitute culture as an alternative to religion and as a bulwark against moral and social anarchy. Culture (and this he defined as 'getting to know . . . the best which has been thought and said in the world') could, he felt, raise men up to a standard of ethical and moral nobility, in which state to do right would be instinctive. In his own words it would result in 'endless growth in wisdom and beauty' and carried away by his enthusiasm for the ensuing 'sweetness and light', he asserted that culture 'goes beyond religion, as religion is generally conceived by us'. In retrospect it all has a cosy and

---

[3] Jarry carried his protest to its logical (or illogical) end by deliberately drinking himself to death at the age of thirty-four, having gravitated from alcohol to ether. It is significant however that interest in Jarry (and also in De Sade with whom Jarry shared certain characteristics) has grown in recent years and in 1948 a 'College of Pataphysics' was founded in his honour.

[4] *The Modern Temper* (New York, 1956), pp. 45, 46.

alluring appeal and, who knows, perhaps it might even have worked. Both Huxley and Arnold, however (although the latter does reveal something of it in his poetry) appeared to have been unaware of the devastating practical implications of a God-less cosmos, in which men and women were answerable only to themselves and to human society.

Albert Camus saw the knowledge of a purposeless world as providing the genesis of the Nazi movement, and in the fourth of his *Letters to a German Friend* (1944) he wrote :

> You never believed in the meaning of this world and you therefore deduce the idea that *everything was equivalent* and *that good and evil could be defined according to one's wishes*. You supposed that in the absence of any human or divine code the only values were those of the animal world – in other words, violence and cunning . . . And, to tell the truth, I, believing I thought as you did, saw no valid argument to answer you except a fierce love of justice which, after all, seemed to me as unreasonable as the most sudden passion. [My italics]

Just as it would be ridiculous to assume that the British ploughman, or for that matter the average country squire, of the early eighteenth century was aware of, or even affected by, Newtonian physics, or the ensuing concept of an ordered universe, the knowledge of which gradually seeped down to the populace at large from the writing and conversations of a small, literate minority, so the cumulative effect of the scientific theories of the nineteenth and twentieth centuries, epitomized by the discoveries and work of Lyell, Darwin, Freud, Pavlov and Einstein, did not immediately manifest itself in broad, social terms. Arnold might mourn that fate had made him a wanderer 'between two worlds, one dead, the other powerless to be born'; Tennyson railed against a 'life as futile, then, as frail', but it was Eliot who showed his generation of the nineteen-twenties 'fear in a handful of dust', and gave to the world the eerie music of 'voices singing out of empty cisterns and exhausted wells'. It is almost impossible to exaggerate the influence and importance of *The Waste Land,* that unrelenting expression of death-in-life which was first published in 1922, to be followed three years later by the equally sombre and expressively entitled poem *The Hollow Men.* Writing of the former, Rose Macaulay recalled its first impact on her generation :

Beyond and through the dazzling, puzzling technique, the
verbal fascination, the magpie glitter of the borrowed and
adapted phrases that brought a whole chorus of literature
into service, enriching and extending every theme – beyond
and through all this there was the sharp sense of recognition. Here was the landscape one knew, had always known;
here were the ruins in the soul.

In retrospect Eliot's subsequent religious conversion seems
inevitable; apart from emulating Jarry and committing suicide
he could proceed no further with his devastating anatomiz-
ation of the predicament of contemporary man, root-less,
faith-less and, in any ultimate sense, aim-less. And the voice
of the early Eliot is the authentic voice of the twentieth-
century intellectual and its message, aided by the advent of
the cinema, television, radio and easily available paperback,
has permeated the contemporary arts, including the 'entertainment' field. The message is not clear nor undistorted, but
it does nevertheless, appear to evince a probably sub-conscious
dislike for, and even in certain cases hatred of, the very
intellect which gave it birth. Since I have treated the whole
subject of the sado-masochistic element in contemporary
culture at length in *Trousered Apes* I shall content myself
here with suggesting that it might be a salutary exercise for
a reader to pursue, in parallel manner, John Barth's *Giles
Goat-Boy* and Henry Fielding's *Tom Jones*; Genet's *The
Balcony* and Goldsmith's *She Stoops to Conquer*; Eliot's *The
Waste Land* and Johnson's *The Vanity of Human Wishes.*
    Each of these three 'pairs' deals, roughly speaking, with
a similar subject or facet of human nature. The two novels
by Barth and Fielding are concerned with sexuality and the
things of the flesh; the plays of Genet and Goldsmith with
deception in one form or another; the poems by Eliot and
Johnson with the condition (universal and perennial, or so
they conceived it) of man. The difference in the tone and
mood is, however, striking and reading the three twentieth-
century writers one becomes aware of a lack; the breezy
good humour and redemptive tolerance of man and his foibles
which characterize the writings of Fielding and Goldsmith
are replaced in those of their modern counterparts with a
viciousness and a hatred and contempt for man and his
posturings. Johnson might write that 'life protracted is protracted woe', but unlike *The Waste Land,* his poem, after

demolishing the vain hopes of finding any true or lasting happiness in this life, concludes with the religious admonition to the reader to trust in God and abide by His decisions which Johnson, in a comparatively rare flash of optimism, suggests are essentially beneficent :

> Implore his aid, in his decision rest,
> Secure whate'er he gives, he gives the best.[5]

These lines are strongly reminiscent of the following from the *Essay on Man,* in which Pope suggests that the reader should *submit* to the eternal plan of what he styles, in another work, the 'Great First Cause' :

> Cease then, nor order imperfection name;
> Our proper bliss depends on what we blame.
> Know thy own point : This kind, this due degree
> Of Blindness, weakness, Heaven bestows on thee.[6]

These lines are followed by perhaps the most controversial of the entire poem :

> All Nature is but art *unknown to thee,*
> All chance, direction which *thou canst not see;*
> All discord, harmony *not understood;*
> All partial evil, universal good;
> And, spite of *pride,* in erring *reason's* spite
> One truth is clear, Whatever is, is right.[7]

[My italics]

The vehement opposition which the message in these lines can provoke was demonstrated vividly to me when I was lecturing on Pope at an American university some years ago. As I concluded reading them, and before I had time to comment on them or attempt an explication, an undergraduate at the back of the room leapt to his feet and shouted angrily : 'How dare you say such things!' It was with great difficulty that he was finally persuaded that I, personally, had not to the best of my knowledge (even in a previous incarnation) been guilty of such a heinous offence as he attributed to their composer, although, to his credit, for the remainder of our time at the university he never failed to eye me with profound suspicion.

---

[5] *The Vanity of Human Wishes,* line 355–356.
[6] I, 281–284.
[7] I, 289–294.

Much of his anger undoubtedly arose from the somewhat offensive complacency of the last line, a complacency that a quarter of a century later Voltaire, outraged by the meaningless slaughter occasioned by the Lisbon earthquake, mercilessly satirized in *Candide*. Some of it, however, I suspect arose from the *submission* which the lines demand of mankind, and also from the intellectual myopia which Pope, convinced of the finitude of human intellect (excepting, perhaps, his own) attributes to men.

Yet herein lies another strange paradox. It may be true, as Krutch suggests, that if 'the plays and the novels of today deal with littler people and less mighty emotions it is not because we have become interested in commonplace souls and their unglamorous adventures but because we have come, willy-nilly, to see the soul of man as commonplace and its emotions as mean.'[8] At the same time, modern man is far less prepared than his ancestors to accept that his mind is finite. His scientific and technological 'advances' have been so astonishingly rapid that he is reluctant to admit that there are areas of human thought and endeavour, such as metaphysics and theology, which remain at best speculative, and in which hardly any appreciable progress has been made.

Thus the intellect is glorified when it produces something of seeming utility but doubted and abhorred by many 'intellectuals' of a humanist persuasion, because its fruits appear to be a realization of a purposeless world wherein human activities are reduced (if that is even the right word) to the level of an ant-heap. Science has improved the physical well-being of mankind immeasurably, and it would be a churlish and foolish ingrate who would wish to return to mediaeval plumbing or to endure an operation without the comforts of anaesthesia; yet at the same time it has *seemed* to reveal a particularly chill and comfortless vista for those of a reflective mind. Perhaps this is what Robert Frost (ever hostile to materialism) had in mind when he wrote :

With a lantern that wouldn't burn
In too frail a buggy we drove
Behind too heavy a horse
Through a pitch-dark limitless grove.

8 *The Modern Temper*, p. 82.

And a man came out of the trees
And took our horse by the head
And reaching back to his ribs
Deliberately stabbed him dead. . . .

(The Draft Horse)

Is there a way out of this seeming *impasse* without sacrificing the intellect (which St Ignatius Loyola declared was
the ultimate sacrifice demanded by God of man), or must new
discoveries continue to benefit us materially while impoverish-
ing us spiritually? Nor should this be regarded as an academic
question. Dr Viktor Frankl of the University of Vienna
Medical School has drawn attention to the paramount fact
that those who *survived* the horrors of the German concen-
tration camps (and he was in four of them, himself) were those
who could look 'towards a *meaning* to fulfil in the future'.
He proceeds :

> I would go one step further and say that the survival value
> of a will to meaning applies to mankind as a whole. I
> believe there is hope for mankind's survival only as long as
> or as soon as people will arrive at the awareness of a
> common denominator in axiological terms; values and
> meanings they might have in common; values and mean-
> ings that might be shared by people and peoples. In other
> words there is hope for mankind's survival provided that
> mankind will be united *by a common will to a common
> meaning*.[9]

I am well aware that this whole question of 'meaning'
has been probed, discussed and debated for countless cen-

---

[9] 'Man in Search of Meaning', Commencement Address, Rockford
College, May 14, 1972. The following by Jung lends additional
support to Frankl's position : 'I should like to call attention to the
following facts. During the past thirty years, people from all the
civilized countries of the earth have consulted me. Many hundreds
of patients have passed through my hands, the greater number being
Protestants, a lesser number Jews, and not more than five or six
believing Catholics. Among all my patients in the second half of life –
that is to say, over thirty-five years – there has not been one whose
problem in the last resort was not that of finding a religious outlook
on life. It is safe to say that every one of them fell ill because he had
lost what the living religions of every age have given to their followers,
and none of them has been really healed who did not regain his
religious outlook. This of course has nothing whatever to do with a
particular creed or membership of a church.' *Psychology and Religion:
West and East*; Volume 11, Bollingen Series XX, Princeton University Press, p. 334.

turies, but there it remains, even amongst the most affluent peoples and societies, mocking their material prosperity and diurnal activities, with a perpetual and persistent 'Why?' Politicians may exhort us to export or import goods, may institute welfare states, concern themselves with the poor and elderly; alternatively they may wage wars, oppress and extort, torture and imprison – but soon all such activities are part of the past and become relegated to the history books. The humanist may well rebuke me at this stage and point out that the *present* state of civilization which we enjoy is the result of cumulative struggles in the past against tyranny, disease, ignorance and poverty, both of mind and spirit. He might press his point home and observe that whatever sophistication my work may contain, together with the material surroundings in which it is being composed – the chair and the desk at which I sit, the pen and paper which I am using, the books on the shelves surrounding the study – all these are real and are the result of such cumulative struggles which men call progress. 'Is all this not enough,' he might ask, 'why should one concern oneself with any ultimate beyond the savouring of here and now?'

I am certainly not unaware of the temporal conveniences and pleasures which surround my life, but I am also at certain times aware of their ephemeral qualities. One might say that the essential tragedy of the perennial human condition is that man is *intellectually* aware of the relentless passage of time, and yet is impotent to affect its course in any way. Both the humanist and myself are equally subject to what Edith Sitwell (writing of Dylan Thomas) called 'the conquering hand of time'. The following by Thomas himself, written when he was twenty-four, expresses the full anguish that follows such realization :

In the groin of the natural doorway I crouched like a tailor
Sewing a shroud for a journey
By the light of the *meat-eating sun*
Dressed to die, the sensual strut begun . . .   [My italics]

Here the poet indicates that even in the womb ('the natural doorway') the embryonic creature is destined for only one inevitable end – 'the shroud'. This is also the theme of Thomas's best-known poem, *Fern Hill*, in which the glory of childhood is seen by the poet to reside in the fact that the child is unaware that he is a prisoner of Time, which will neverthless be his eventual destroyer: 'Time held me *green* and *dying*/Though I sang in my chains like the sea.' (My italics) Even when we say or write the word 'now', the moment is already past and we are confronted with another 'now', equally evanescent and ungraspable. We all resemble passengers in a coach which has only one destination. We fondly imagine that there will be certain points on the journey when the coach will stop, allowing us to alight and picnic on the green sward; that, however briefly, time will stop and allow us to savour the 'now' of our existence, but the coach rolls on, some stoically accepting the fact, others screaming hysterically, still others stifling the knowledge in drink or drugs or frenzied activity, while a dwindling minority continues to nurse a hope that at their journey's end they will find the green sward of *eternal* consolation – that permanency denied them in real life. The implications of the foregoing caused C. S. Lewis to write as follows in *God in the Dock*:

> It is not Christianity which need fear the giant universe. It is those systems which place the whole meaning of existence in biological or social evolution on our own planet. It is the creative evolutionist, the Bergsonian or Shavian, or the Communist, who should tremble when he looks up at the night sky. For he really is committed to a sinking ship. He really is attempting to ignore the discovered nature of things, as though by concentrating on the possibly upward trend in a single planet he could make himself forget the inevitable downward trend in the universe as a whole, the trend to low temperatures and irrevocable disorganization. For entropy is the real cosmic wave, and evolution only a momentary tellurian ripple within it.

This is what the hymnologist, F. H. Lyte, had in mind when he wrote:

> Change and decay in all around I see;
> O Thou, who *changest not*, abide with me.

The transiency of this life is inescapably and logically irrefutable,[10] but how should it affect us and to what extent should it influence our daily lives? Obviously, to dwell on it to the exclusion of other thoughts would be to invite excessive morbidity and total quietism. To ignore it, however, is to fall

---

[10] Even if one attempted to refute it, the refutation itself would take place within a time-span composed of passing moments.

into the dangers of facile and unthinking ameliorism, and to become a prey to the equally spurious political creeds of various persuasions which seek to induce men to believe that a heaven on earth is just around the corner, providing we vote this way or that, or endure a few million deaths to secure some secular utopia. Such beliefs have always been present and have directly or indirectly been responsible for that most pernicious of all creeds – that the End justifies the Means. But what 'End'? Even if, magically, all wars ceased, economic and social equality became overnight a reality, cancer and other diseases susceptible to cure, man would still be mortal and consequently subject to the consciousness of a fleeting succession of evanescent experiences.

Obviously, therefore, a *balanced* view of human life would reject both excessive materialism (recognizing the ephemeral fruits of such, and suspicious of any secular creed based exclusively on the here and now) while at the same time realizing that the human experience can and does embrace certain joyful, life-enhancing experiences and that these can be savoured without hypercritical analysis.

I suggested in *Trousered Apes* apropos of *excessive* and *exclusive* materialism on the one hand, and *excessive* and *exclusive* rationalism on the other, that both lead to the same nihilistic terminus and that a synthesis of these would seem to offer the best hope for the future of man. Perhaps critics will accuse me of being addicted to the middle way, but I should like to suggest in the present work that a combination of the spiritual and the temporal would seem once again, to afford the individual human spirit a philosophically responsible and at the same time workable creed. We can recognize the transient quality of *all* human experiences without creating a morbid religion of it, and can agree with Keats that 'Joy' does indeed have 'his hand ever at his lips, bidding adieu', without thereby denying the very existence of joy or indulging in what John Donne styled 'a borrowing of misery'. Man does not live by thought alone, and it would be an exceptionally cloistered and malignant philosopher who would think or wish otherwise.

Implicit in the passage by Krutch which constitutes the epigraph to this chapter ('[man's] religions are fair and wonderful to him alone') is a denial of the possibility of a controlling, cosmic intelligence – in other words, God. (In fairness to Krutch, in a subsequent book, *The Measure of Man,*

E

he does draw different conclusions although retaining his basic analysis and description.) Yet this paramount factor would seem to determine whether man regards himself as a creature of divine origin and purpose or simply another, more intelligent form of animal life.

Yet it cannot be both ways. Either a controlling force exists and gives meaning and significance to the universe and to individual and collective human life, or else, as Tennyson expressed it:

> Earth is darkness at the core
> And dust and ashes all that is.

The existentialist[11] regards the earth and the entire universe as essentially random, accidental, and therefore meaningless phenomena, devoid of any significance or morality.

Man, however, apparently does retain a measure of choice. When confronted by this cosmic inanity, he can decided either 'to lead an enthusiastic and honourable existence', or he can laspe into despair. The atheistic basis of such a philosophy is too evident to need any elaboration, but certain questions remain unanswered. When confronted by such overwhelming chaos on all sides, why should man bother to make a choice, particularly since in any ultimate sense all such decisions are meaningless and futile? Jean-Paul Sartre appears to have reached this spiritual nadir in *Saint Genet*, when he declares that even after we have made our commitment and decision we are still 'impossible nullities'.

Tennyson, it seems to me, had a much more logical and honest reaction to the problem. After contemplating the possibility of such a meaningless, soulless universe, he declared:

> 'Twere hardly worth my while to choose
> Of things all mortal, or to use
> A little patience ere I die;
> 'Twere best at once to sink in peace,
> Like birds the charming serpent draws,
> To drop head-foremost in the jaws,
> Of vacant darkness and to cease.

The fact that Sartre and his followers do not pursue

---

[11] I am not referring here to such 'religious existentialists' as Gabriel Marcel, Martin Buber, Karl Jaspers and Paul Tillich, but rather to that type of existentialism typified by Jean-Paul Sartre.

Tennyson's course suggests either that they have not faced up to the full implication of their beliefs, or that they have discovered some palliative, such as communism, in the furtherance of which creed they can escape, at least temporarily, from the knowledge of the futility of absolutely everything, including, of course, the futility of whichever fashionable escapist activity currently holds their attention.

Such a philosophy may sustain itself for a time, living on its own dynamism, but eventually the persistent, questioning 'why?' will arise, and with no adequate answer the edifice must crumble.

Non-religious activities resemble players in a football game in which there are no rules, no referee, no time limit, and no spectators. For a time a certain physical exuberance will keep the participants occupied, but as their energy becomes sapped, so gradually they will realize the purposelessness of the whole game.

One by one they will retire, leaving only the totally unintelligent and insensitive to continue in the endless farce. As Pierre Teilhard de Chardin has written :

> Even on stacks of material energy, even under the spur of immediate fear or desire, without the taste for life, mankind would soon stop inventing and constructing for a work it knew to be doomed in advance. . . . If progress is a myth, that is to say, if faced by the work involved we can say : What's the good of it all?' our efforts will flag.[12]

Even if we adopt an optimistic attitude and assume that we have the technological means to avert and control the appalling consequences attendant on over-population, and other environmental threats, we can only accomplish this through an undreamed-of spirit of co-operation and personal and national selflessness.

Such sacrifices will only be forthcoming if, in Teilhard's words, we retain that 'taste for life', that belief so rapidly being eroded today, that modern man is more than a trousered ape, that somewhere deep inside him is something unique, call it a soul if you will, that defies all the attempts to reduce him to a remarkably aggressive and hypocritical primate.

To quote from Teilhard again :

---

[12] *The Phenomenon of Man,* tr. Bernard Wall (London, 1959), pp. 232, 233.

Either there is an escape from death – somewhere – for
an individual's thought, for his self-consciousness, or else
the world is a hideous mistake. And if it is, then there
is no use in us going on. But, since the uselessness of going
on is an idea intolerable to everyone, the alternative must
be to believe. To awaken this belief shall be, now more
than ever, my task.[13]

Teilhard is dead, but the task remains. And it has an
urgency unsurpassed in the entire recorded annals of human
history. Already countless thousands of the young are demon-
strating that they are in fact losing (if they have not already
lost) that essential 'taste for life'. A pervasive death-wish is
inherent in much of contemporary literature and life, disguised under various forms of nihilism and 'protests against
the cosmos'.

There are, it would appear, two methods in which it is
possible at least to challenge the assumption of an absurd
universe, and therefore the ultimate absurdity of collective
and individual human life. The first involves the finitude of
the human mind. Plato declared that God, as ideal Being,
and not man, is the measure of all things; and when the Lord
out of the whirlwind rebuked Job it was in terms that stressed
man's presumption at attempting to understand His infinite
purpose :

Where wast thou when I laid the foundations of the
earth? declare, if thou hast understanding.
Who hath laid the measures therof, if thou knowest?
or who hath stretched the line upon it? *Job*, xxxviii, 4

As I have suggested elsewhere a cat or other domestic pet
may be induced to focus its eyes upon a newspaper picture
of other cats, a mirror, or upon some other object which
might reasonably be expected to arouse its interest. The result
is invariably disappointing. The cat may look at the picture
but it obviously does not 'see' it in a human sense. It exhibits
no interest whatsoever. Does this mean that the picture has
no message, that it is meaningless and absurd, or is it not
simply that the cat is physically incapable of finding any
meaning in it because of some innate deficiency in its per-
ceptory apparatus? And may not man be similarly myopic
when he contemplates the cosmos, yet through pride refuse

---

[13] Quoted in Claude Cuénot, *Teilhard de Chardin*, tr. Vincent
Colimore (Baltimore, 1965), p. 158.

to admit this possibility? There are, after all, countless sounds which evade the human ear because of an innate inability of that organ to pick them up, and yet they do exist. This argument does not prove the existence of order but at least leaves the question open to conjecture and faith.

The second approach offers a more persuasive challenge to non-belief and is familiar to readers of Teilhard and Whitehead. Briefly, it proceeds as follows. Most scientists agree that 'in the beginning' there was a molten fiery ball destined to become man's habitat – the earth. Over countless millions of years a cooling process took place, eventually leading to that state when waters covered the 'face of the deep'.[15] Through a process imperfectly understood, eventually tiny single cells appeared in this water and by a seemingly inexorable process began to join and complexify.[14] This process of complexification, and additivity, continued unabated until finally and miraculously appeared a creature *capable of the rudiments of thought* – ancestral man. In Teilhard's own words 'thought is born'. Now, since it is axiomatic that nothing can come from nothing, such thought must have been latent or embryonic in that original molten ball. To quote Teilhard again : 'In the world, nothing could ever burst forth as final across the different thresholds successively traversed by evolution (however critical they may be) which has not already existed in an obscure and primordial way.'[16] The genesis of such thought, however, remains the greatest mystery of them all, a miracle transcending any others performed on this earth. A materialist may suggest that what is here called 'thought' is simply a complex interaction of electrical impulses, but this in no way reduces the mystery, for the brain which he uses to invalidate or diminish the theory is itself only a similar collection of electrical impulses, and it does not greatly matter whether that

---

[14] Sir Julian Huxley describes the process as 'a passage of subatomic units to atoms, from atoms to inorganic and later to organic molecules, thence to the first subcellular living units or self-replicating assemblages of molecules, and then to cells, to multicellular individuals, to cephalized metazoa with brains, to primitive man and now to civilized societies.' Intro. to *The Phenomenon of Man* (London 1959), p. 15.
[15] An alternative opinion is that the earth began through aggregation of cool matter with subsequent internal heating. This theory in no way invalidates the argument which follows.
[16] *The Phenomenon of Man,* p. 71.

collection is styled 'thought' or not. It is what I am using at
the moment to create these words and what the reader, again
miraculously, is using to absorb and interpret them. It would
appear that eventually either to refute or to accept the fact
that this mystery exists may be a matter of temperament and
will. In other words, what William James called a decision
for our 'passional nature', as opposed to a logical preference.

Although, as Teilhard points out, man is physically very
much an animal, 'so little separable anatomically from the
anthropoids that the modern classifications made by zoologists
return to the position of Linnaeus and include him with them
in the same super-family, the hominidae',[17] yet he is a being
filled with qualities which set him dramatically apart from
all other creatures. He, alone, has developed the capacity for
sympathy and empathy; the ability to communicate abstract
ideas and theories; to delight in small creatures such as
puppies or kittens which would be merely prey for most other
carnivores; to appreciate a sunset or a sonnet; to frame laws
that regulate social intercourse and forbid violence, theft and
murder. He has evolved mathematical formulae and stepped
on the surface of the moon. His powers of invention have
produced telescopes capable of detecting stars and nebulae so
distant that his lagging imagination can only conceive of
them in light-years, and microscopes which reveal a world so
infinitely small that he has to fall back on metaphoric language to describe it. All of this is the product of his thought-
processes, latent in that molten fiery ball, and yet deep inside
him, where his true being resides, there is an ache and a
void. He is not totally at home in the world which these
thought-processes, transferred into reflection or action, have
created. 'Every beast', wrote Johnson in *Rasselas*, 'that strays
beside me has the same corporal necessities with myself; he is
hungry and crops the grass, he is thirsty and drinks from the
stream, his thirst and hunger are appeased, he is satisfied and
sleeps . . . I am hungry and thirsty like him, but when thirst
and hunger cease I am not at rest; I am, like him, pained
with want, but am not, like him, satisfied with fullness.'

What follows has been germinating in my mind for some
considerable time but its seeming extravagance has hitherto
prohibited me from committing it to paper. Recent scientific
discoveries and hypotheses, however, have suggested that

---

[17] *The Phenomenon of Man*, p. 163.

Blake's statement – 'What is now proved was once only imagin'd' – still holds true and this is, pedhaps, a justification.

It may be recalled that when Satan in *Paradise Lost* has volunteered to undertake the perilous journey to Earth, there to attempt to seduce 'the puny inhabitants', Adam and Eve, away from God, he proceeds to the gates of Hell where sit two terrifying creatures, Sin and Death. After a somewhat curious family reunion (Sin is a product of his mind and Death the offspring of their passion), he bribes Sin to unlock the gates and looks out onto 'a dark/illimitable ocean without bound,/without dimension; where length, breadth and highth,/and time and place are lost.' (II, 891-894). Satan, who certainly lacks neither courage nor audacity, surveys this scene with some considerable trepidation, 'pondering his voyage' – the first recorded space-flight. Milton then proceeds to describe in greater detail the prospect which the 'arch-fiend' is contemplating :

> Into this wild abyss,
> *The womb of Nature and perhaps her grave,*
> Of neither sea, nor shore, nor air, nor fire,
> But all these in their pregnant causes mixed
> Confusedly, and which thus must ever fight
> Unless the Almighty Maker them ordain
> His dark materials to create more worlds,
> Into this wild abyss the wary Fiend
> Stood on the brink of Hell and looked awhile
> Pondering his voyage.
>
> (II, 910–919. My italics)

These words, presumably remotely derived from the first chapter of Genesis ('And the earth was without form, and void') as well as from Hesiod, Herodotus and other writers of antiquity, have haunted me ever since I first read them as a schoolboy, and they seemed (and still seem) to embody in a prophetic way some truth which Milton apprehended in mystic fashion and which he attempted to clothe in words. During the past few years, astronomers have discovered what are described as 'black holes' in the universe. These are regions of space where the remains of once giant stars have disappeared completely out of 'our' universe, leaving no trace. The question arising from this is how matter can simply cease to exist? In other words, where has it gone? Some theorists believe that it is sucked into what Professor John A. Wheeler of Princeton University has called 'Superspace' – the universe which lasts for ever – 'the womb of Nature and perhaps her grave'. Black holes accordingly could be regarded as the entrances to eternity.

I realize that at this point I am indulging in wild conjecture and yet the thought persistently recurs. It must be at least *possible* that man's anguished awareness of the *transiency* of human life and his yearning for permanency, expressed in his valiant but pathetic attempts to endow a timeless quality to impermanent artifacts and emotions, together with his feelings of alienation – that inner ache which seemingly separates him from all other creatures – all of these *could* be explained by a yearning to return to the womb of thought – eternity. Let me at this stage attempt to pull certain strands in the hypothesis logically together. If (and I stress that it is only hypothetical) such 'superspace' exists (and it is at present a strong contender to explain the existence of 'black holes'), then our universe and our world in an unimaginably distant past have emerged from it. As we have seen earlier the molten fiery ball, this world, latently or potentially contained the power of thought. The *ultimate* source of such thought, however, would be that eternal and changeless 'superspace' into which *eventually,* and again in an unimaginably distant future, our entire galaxy will (according to Wheeler) 'go swirling down a time tunnel in space, like water gurgling out of the bath'. This would be a physical, and ultimately a theological manifestation of 'Alpha and Omega, the beginning and the ending . . . which is, and which was, and is to come.'

Albert Camus, one of the most intelligent and sensitive of twentieth-century philosophers, concluded his examination of an 'absurd' world by declaring that in judging it absurd he had been too hasty : 'The absurd is not in man . . . nor in the world, but in their presence *together*.' (My italics.) Would not the hypothesis above help to explain this feeling that the world is somehow inadequate or inappropriate to man's deepest longings and aspirations, resulting in what Tennyson called 'divine despair'? With the evolving and burgeoning of human thought processes, the desire for an ultimate meaning to life is increasing and the more developed and 'sensitive' an individual's mental endowment is, the truer this appears to be.

Appropriately and quintessentially, Keats, that supreme

'romantic', expressed the desire to return to the ultimate
source of being in his *Ode To A Nightingale* :

> Darkling I listen; and, for many a time
> I have been half in love with easeful Death . . .
> Now more than ever seems it rich to die,
> To cease upon the midnight with no pain,
> While thou art pouring forth thy soul abroad
> In such an ecstasy!

Some readers may feel that such sentiments, expressed by a
tubercular young poet over 150 years ago, are totally irrelevant
and simply indicative on my part of an academic pre-
occupation with matters which belong more properly in a
rarefied journal devoted to literary criticism. While recognizing their right to suspicion, perhaps the following, written
by a sixteen-year-old English schoolboy in 1971, will indicate
that the sentiments are by no means confined to nineteenth-
century poets but are widely prevalent today and give additional support to my earlier contention that the search for
an ultimate meaning has become the dominant pre-occupation
among a growing minority of today's young :

> I spend a great deal of time wondering and worrying
> about the meanings and reasons behind life. I see the
> world as a spaceship – a tiny, insignificant object floating
> through infinity. I can't understand why people have so
> much purpose. If they only thought a bit more like I do
> they might see how tiny they were. We're born without ask-
> ing to be born. We get into the train of life, which takes us
> along a hell-ride to a final escape and peace – death.
> Death is my idea of bliss – not as a paradise, but as a
> nothing.[18]

A 'cult of death' is already incipient in the United States
and seminars on this subject have been introduced on
some campuses. The fundamental question, however, is to
what extent and how should such feelings be repudiated?
Obviously, if I thought life to be meaningless and absurd I
should certainly not compound the absurdity by writing books
or indulging in abstract, philosophic speculation. So far as we
are able to ascertain, man is the sole custodian of thought in
the universe, and this surely confers upon him a responsibility
and a very special sort of dignity. The responsibility, if truly

---

[18] Quoted by Robin Richardson and John Chapman in *Images of
Life,* 1973, p. 129.

E*

comprehended, demands that his thoughts and actions measure up to the uniqueness of his position, exercising the consequent power which he enjoys in a benevolent fashion and recognizing that any enhancement of his own life, or enlargement of his material aspirations, if obtained immoderately at the expense of other forms of life, are defeating not only of self but, ultimately, of his evolutionary mission. The facts regarding the depredations which collectively and individually we have visited, and are continuing to visit, upon this planet, a fertile but delicate oasis in the deserts of surrounding space and our only home, are now only too apparent. To reverse such trends will be neither easy nor comfortable, but I cannot believe that mankind will supinely preside over its own demise. 'Great dangers', wrote William McNeill in *The Rise of the West,* 'alone produce great victories, and without the possibility of failure, all human achievements would be savourless. Our world assuredly lacks neither dangers nor the possibility of failure. It also offers a theatre for heroism such as has seldom or never been seen before in all history.'[19]

It has been my intention in writing this book neither to gloss over the dangers of our present physical and spiritual situation, nor to suggest that it is too late for action. Civilization may, as Toynbee has suggested, be in 'the eleventh hour', but it is not yet too late providing informed and concerned persons, and especially those engaged in the education of the young, resolve to declare a moratorium on pettiness, factionalism and ideological differences and unite in what is surely the greatest and most urgent 'cause' of all; the preservation of thought and its sole custodian – man.

---

[19] Chicago, 1963, p. 807.

EPILOGUE*

None but the totally moronic, depraved, insensitive or myopically self-centred individual can contemplate the contemporary scene with anything other than profound anxiety and foreboding. As one looks ahead, one is reminded of the traveller who, having visited Los Angeles, remarked on his return, 'I have seen the future and it doesn't work'.

Only a few years ago, this would have seemed an eccentric minority view, but far too many eminent men and women are today questioning the basic structure of a society increasingly characterized by wars, civil strife, pollution, urban neurosis, over-population, strikes, gross materialism, exploitation and inflation for those concerned to be designated as 'cranks'. As a highly intelligent undergraduate remarked to me a year or two ago: 'The past is irrelevant and the future unthinkable'.

Although undoubtedly many of our ills can be attributed to our post-lapsarian condition and to the perennial folly inherent in human nature, yet at the same time educational theory and practice must bear some of the responsibility for the sort of world we are living in and creating for our children. With the growing secularization of our schools, teacher-training colleges and universities, 'cleverness' has become the sole aim and criterion of many teachers. But the history of the twentieth century provides far too many glaring examples of hideous atrocities committed by highly intelligent 'devils' for there to be any complacency regarding this present trend. As Jon Wynne-Tyson expresses it in *The Civilised Alternative*:

> What we have not sufficiently woken up to as yet is that while doing away with the ritual and dogma of organized religion, we also deprived ourselves of the essential discipline – and consequently comfort – of those moral guide-lines that have lain hidden like veins and arteries in the all too fleshly body of the established church.

---

* This chapter is an attempt to provide a synopsis of the main arguments advanced; such a resumé may prove helpful insofar as it clarifies the writer's basic intentions, giving the reader, in capsulated and convenient form, the general purport of the book.

Cardinal Newman defined a truly great intellect as 'one which takes a connected view of old and new, past and present, far and near and which has an insight into the influence of all these, one on another.' His concept of a university was that of an intellectual institution performing for the mind the same function as a gymnasium does for the body – in other words to exercise the *whole* intellect.

No healthy man in his right senses would attend a gymnasium daily for the *sole* purpose of exercising his right arm or his left leg to the absolute neglect of his other limbs. If such a physical programme were followed, he would end up with one limb functioning perfectly, while the others would be hopelessly withered and weak – in short, he would be a cripple. Mentally, over-specialization, particularly in the physical sciences, has resulted in a similar crippling of our entire society – in a paradoxical, absurd civilization which has lost direction and meaning because the parts no longer function for the ultimate good of the whole. Moreover, it is one of those tragic ironies of our age that, just at the moment when the problems of the environment are seen to be inextricably related, university specialists (and indeed specialists in all walks of life) are becoming ever more specialized.

Meanwhile, the corpus of technology in indeed terrifyingly cumulative and can be, and is being handed down intact from generation to generation. The wisdom to control this knowledge, however, has to be painfully re-acquired through experience and study by each successive generation; the resulting imbalance has created a society which I have described in *Trousered Apes* as one consisting of 'technological giants and moral pygmies'.

When the team under the direction of Rutherford split the atom at Cambridge in 1932, it was a superb example of scientific cleverness and ability. Only one totally unacquainted with the horrors of Nagasaki and Hiroshima could claim, however, that mankind was ethically, or morally, equipped to handle the seemingly inevitable extension and application of Rutherford's work.

If this was true of the atom bomb, how much more so is it of the myriad discoveries which have taken place in the physical sciences, particularly biology, in the past twenty years. Referring to these, Alvin Toffler, the author of *Future Shock,* writes: 'the nature of what can and will be done exceeds anything that man is as yet psychologically or morally prepared to live with.'

A short time ago, on a television programme devoted to a discussion on the rôle of the teacher, an eminent British educationist declared that the aims of the teacher should be to sow doubts in the minds of his pupils. This is of course simply an extension of scientific empiricism and philosophic scepticism to the field of education, but surely this view (and it is shared by many teachers and educationalists) if carried to its logical conclusion, makes no sense whatsoever. As G. K. Chesterton observed : 'The only reason for having an open mind is the same as having an open mouth; so that eventually one can bite on something.'

The philosophic theories of the present age tend to assume that 'discussion' is by definition a good thing, and therefore the more children can be taught to disagree with previously-held notions, the more active their brains must be. The classroom, therefore, becomes a more stimulating place, vibrating with intellectual energy. However, as Walter Bagehot observed in the nineteenth century, 'an age of discussion' is an age when the 'cake of custom, the chief preserving force in a society, has been broken.' What we are witnessing today is an age of discussion, a critical period in which loud disputes are accompanied by generally weak conclusions. Diagnosticians abound, but one looks in vain for anyone prepared to *prescribe* for the social, political and educational maladies of which anyone of sensitivity must be only too aware. Instead of the present hiatus which characterizes the contemporary scene, I am making bold to suggest that there is a desperate need for some educational theory which will be seen to be axiomatic and comparable to an Euclidean theorem in geometry. Something to which all men of goodwill and good sense, will be prepared to give their assent and thereafter their wholehearted effort and allegiance. With this end in view, may I tentatively suggest that the survival of the species is paramount and supersedes, or should supersede, all other factional or other priorities. As Yehudi Menuhin recently wrote in a letter :

> Any narrowing of the broader motive carries with it the need to act against the particular, in other words against the remainder. If one does not include in some way the whole of living existence on our planet in one's basic attitudes and morality, one finds oneself acting on behalf of

one part against another. Perhaps this dilemma can be resolved by learning to accept oneself as the first and final material to be conquered, not 'they', or 'it', 'him' or 'her', but 'us' above all 'myself'. To improve the dreams and to raise the sights of all of us, including myself, this would seem to be one of the avenues of redemption. There is today no lack of people ready to discipline themselves and sacrifice themselves, but the mistake is that this eternal capacity for self-immolation (along with the immolation of others) is held at the service of partisan causes exclusively, fought with enormous dedication and courage, but almost never on behalf of the enemy or of life in general. The desire to improve oneself materially, and the false spiritual justification employed, seem almost always tied up with the compulsion to destroy others, and the same goes hand in hand with the desire to enjoy, to assert or to castigate. Man can no longer afford to act so blindly today, without bringing desolation on the whole planet. Therefore we must learn to fight for total life and total survival, and against all immediate baser and partisan ends.

If through our folly, we continue on our present Gadarene-like march towards self-extermination, then man will have no one but himself to blame and it will not matter very much who presides over the final extermination of mankind – fascist, communist, Black Panther, Weatherman, IRA – for there will be no one left to record it and the ultimate, Pyrrhic victory by man over man will have been achieved.

What I am proposing, therefore, is firstly the total de-politicization of our educational system. Politics is, as presently conceived and executed, devoid of any moral or ethical dimension, the poor man's philosophy, and as it largely consists of the art of promising and occasionally providing, the populace at large with more and more *materialistic* benefits, thereby creating ever-increasing pollution and other depredations of our already battered planet, it should be repudiated; for anyone with a logical mind can see clearly that a *finite* world cannot go on meeting the demands of often artificially-fanned *infinite* aspirations. Today's luxuries become tomorrow's 'necessities' and such is the nature of man that no sooner has one ambition been gratified than he has to invent some further object on which to fasten his want.

In other words, 'want' is a constant but its projections vary from a bowl of rice to a Velasquez. As I suggested on a recent television discussion programme, the present-day inhabitant of a council house enjoys a higher standard of living in terms of heating, lighting, sanitation and other materialistic goods than did a Tudor monarch. Mr Escot, a character in Peacock's novel *Headlong Hall* (1816) summarized the whole dreary process of unalloyed materialism when he spoke as follows:

> These improvements, as you call them, appear to me only so many links in the great chain of corruption, which will soon fetter the whole human race in irreparable slavery and incurable wretchedness.
>
> Your improvements proceed in a simple ratio, while the factitious wants and unnatural appetites they engender proceed in a compound one; and thus one generation acquires 50 wants, and 50 means of supplying them are invented, which in turn engenders two new ones; so that the next generation has 100, the next 200, the next 400 till every human being becomes such a helpless compound of perverted inclinations that he is altogether at the mercy of external circumstances, loses all independence and single-ness of character and degenerates so rapidly from the primitive dignity of his sylvan origin, that is it is scarcely possible to indulge in any other expectation than that the whole species must at length be exterminated by its own infinite imbecility and vileness.

Eventually, if we are to escape from the materialistic slavery envisioned in the foregoing, then educationally we must attempt to produce a generation whose aims are *cultural* rather than physical and in order to do so, it is necessary that teachers at all levels be agreed on this as a primary and common goal. No doubt certain objections will be raised against such a proposal and those who advocate it will un-doubtedly be accused of authoritarianism and an attempt to brainwash. To such allegations I would reply as follows: firstly, as I have already suggested, the aim of our educational system for the past half-century has been increasingly to *provoke* the individual mind into thought, to foment dis-cussion of, and indeed dissent from, previously held doctrines and dogmas. At the same time, every educated mind is con-vinced that *harmony* between nations is today the indispens-able pre-requisite for man's continued existence on this planet. However, the supra-individualism of our educational goals scarcely coincides with the social consensus which we demand on a global scale. In other words, it seems that, logically, such a consensus must be obtained, or else we drift in helpless 'discussion' towards the inevitable destruction of the entire eco-system. Secondly, World War II, in addition to the hideous slaughter and mass destruction of much that was precious, left an additional cruel legacy which has paralyzed much of Western thought. Because the Nazi régime was authoritarian, an increasing rejection of *all* authority has resulted and anyone accused of exercising control is facilely, but damagingly, accused of being a fascist. However, as Edmund Burke wrote in 1791 :

> Men are qualified for civil liberty in exact proportion to their disposition to put moral chains upon their own appetites . . . Society cannot exist unless a controlling power upon will and appetite be placed somewhere, and the less of it there is within, the more there is without. It is ordained in the eternal constitution of things that men of intemperate minds cannot be free. Their passions forge their fetters.

Moreover, such is the appetitive nature of man that, if left to his own devices, he will undoubtedly demand more and more. Again, therefore, it would seem that if we are to survive, *someone* at *some time* must attempt the diversion to cultural goals which I have outlined above, and if this is not done by individual self-control (and such self-control can only come as a result of educating people to the full implications of their actions) then it will either be done through a form of benevolent despotism or if, left too late, by a malevolent one.

As Ruskin wrote :

> Education is not so much a matter of teaching a pupil to know what he did not previously know; rather it is a matter of teaching him to behave as he did not previously behave.

Perhaps I ought to make it clear at this point that what I am proposing is not tantamount to Illich's 'de-schooling.' Although his ideas do posit a challenge to all educationalists, like all radical suggestions (of the right or left) they do contain a fatal flaw. Illich is himself a product of an educational system which, whatever its manifest deficiencies may be, gave him a sense of 'concern' without which he would not have been moved to voice his thoughts. What I am suggesting is rather 're-schooling'.

Given the above premises, it is curious that we have never sufficiently investigated the possibilities of *rediscovery* in our educational programmes as an adequate substitute for discovery, and as a possible source of intellectual satisfaction.

As a teacher of seventeenth- and eighteenth-century literature (and consequently of the philosophy, history and theology of those periods), I am constantly gratified and amazed at the reactions of today's undergraduates to the religious and philosophical theories expounded in Milton's *Paradise Lost* and Pope's *Essay on Man,* to cite just two examples. It is as if a new planet had suddenly entered their vision, and their intellectual excitement at such a 'novel' cosmic and social view is both stimulating and encouraging. (I am particularly interested in their reactions to the belief commonly held in the past, in the value of collective and cumulative, as opposed to individual wisdom. This is so contrary to the contemporary cult of 'doing your own thing' that it affords an opportunity to indicate, from an environmental viewpoint, the social irresponsibility and cant of the current slogan.) To those who would question the relevance of such studies, I would suggest that nothing is more vital to our frenzied, open-nerved culture than to recapture something of that golden mean, with emphasis upon moderate ambitions (together with the insistence that man's overweening pride was at the root of most of his problems) which the writers, theologians and philosophers of the eighteenth century both preached and seriously attempted to practice.

Futhermore, the past has a great deal to offer both in terms of beauty and as a necessary intellectual foil to the present. Contemporary ideas need to be weighed not against others of the same period but against those of the past and it is here that the average modern student is defenceless. He is, as I think most teachers would agree, rooted in what one might call 'temporal provincialism', his interests and leisure reading confined almost totally to contemporary film makers, television pundits, writers and thinkers.

Could not courses in chemistry, physics, biology and mathematics be structured to emphasize their historical and philosophical backgrounds – to subject some of their basic assumptions to a vigorous, critical scrutiny in the context of environmental catastrophe?

The fact that such an approach has not yet been attempted (except perhaps at St. John's College, Maryland) should not prevent a serious examination of the proposal. If adopted, it should certainly curtail, if not extinguish, the suicidal specialization which currently passes for education in most countries. The practical results of this may be symbolized by Dr. Paul Ehrlich's stressing the absolute necessity for population control *now,* while simultaneously organ transplanters in various parts of the world 'strive officiously to keep alive' (with the ultimate hope, presumably, of conferring immortality upon) ever-growing numbers without apparently the least concern for the long-range effects of such experiments on the race between population and food, population and space, population and human dignity. (Marshall McLuhan's definition of a specialist is both provocative and pertinent : 'one who never makes small mistakes while moving towards the grand fallacy'.)

Parts of the foregoing will draw angry rebukes from critics both right and left. The former will allege that such an educational programme would result in shallowness. To this I would simply reply that we cannot as a species afford to go on producing educated men who have every grace except the gift for survival. Moreover, educational standards need not suffer if teachers inculcate a rigorous spirit of scholarship and attainment in pupils towards these suggested interdisciplinary studies. In other words, there is a vital need to construct a syllabus which would indicate the inter-relationship of all knowledge, so that students of all ages grow up in a world which has meaning and significance for them individually and collectively.

The latter will no doubt concentrate on the authoritarian nature of my remarks. This, however, will merely confirm what a growing number of people must by now suspect; namely, that if religion was formerly the opium of the people, politics in the twentieth century has become their heroin, in that it blinkers their vision and results in a comfortably closed mind which acts predictably to all and any situations. The major political parties and trade-unionists, in any democratic country, since they base their appeal on materialistic promises and actively enlarge people's aspirations, resemble yokels at a fairground throwing balls at a coconut-shy while a tornado is rapidly approaching them from the rear.

All the foregoing leads one finally to the crucial question : 'Is man worth saving?' After all, if he is as destructive as ecologists say he is, is he not merely a messy, predatory

mammal and would not nature be better off without him?
In other words, no valid discussion of the hypothetical future
of man can, in the last analysis, ignore the question of
human value. If man is *merely* a 'naked ape', or a 'walking
bag of sea water' as certain scientists choose to regard him,
or a complex but predictable collection of reactions to various
stimuli, as Dr. B. F. Skinner and other behaviourists assert,
then apart from a natural but sentimental loyalty to one's own
species his disappearance from the scene would be of very
little importance in a biological sense and would have no
real significance for any creature or thing other than man
himself. As Joseph Wood Krutch has written :

> [Man's] arts, his religions, and his civilizations – these are
> fair and wonderful things, but they are fair and wonderful
> to him alone. With the extinction of his poetry would come
> also the extinction of the only sensibility for which it has any
> meaning and there would remain nothing capable of
> feeling a loss.

Apparently implicit in Krutch's observation ('his religions are
fair and wonderful to him alone') is a denial of the possibility
of a controlling, cosmic intelligence – in other words, God.
And this factor would seem to determine whether man regards
himself as a creature of divine origin and purpose or simply
another more intelligent, extremely destructive form of animal
life – the ultimate 'killer ape'. Yet it cannot be both ways –
either a controlling force exists and gives meaning and
significance to the universe and to collective and individual
human life, or else, as Tennyson expressed it :

> Earth is darkness at the core
> And dust and ashes all that is.

Atheistic existentialists regard the earth and the entire
universe as essentially random and accidental and therefore
meaningless phenomena devoid of any significance or morality.
Man, however, apparently does retain a measure of choice.
When confronted by this cosmic inanity, he can decide
either to lead an enthusiastic and honourable existence or
he can lapse into despair. The atheistic basis of such a
philosophy is too evident to need any elaboration, but certain
questions remain unanswered. When confronted by such
overwhelming chaos on all sides, why should man bother to
make a choice particularly since in any *ultimate* sense all

such decisions are meaningless and futile? Jean-Paul Sartre appears to have reached this spiritual nadir when, in *Saint Genet*, he declares that even after we have made our commitment and decision, we are still 'impossible nullities'.

Tennyson has a much more logical reaction to the problem. After contemplating the possibility of such a meaningless, soulless universe, he declared :

> 'Twere hardly worth my while to choose
> Of things all mortal, or to use
> A little patience ere I die;
> 'Twere best at once to sink in peace,
> Like birds the charming serpent draws,
> To drop head-foremost in the jaws,
> Of vacant darkness and to cease.

The fact that Sartre and his followers do not pursue Tennyson's course suggests either that they have not faced up to the full implication of their beliefs, or that they have discovered some palliative, such as communism, in the furtherance of which creed they can escape, at least temporarily, from the knowledge of the futility of absolutely *everything* including, of course, the futility of whichever fashionable escapist activity currently holds their attention. Such a philosophy (if philosophy it be) may sustain itself for a *time* living on its own dynamism but eventually the persistent, questioning 'why?' will arise and with no adequate answer the edifice must crumble. Non-believing activists resemble players in a football game in which there are no rules, no referee, no time limit and eventually no spectators. For a certain while physical exuberance will keep the participants occupied, but as their energy becomes sapped, they will realize the purposelessness of the game. One by one they will retire, leaving only the totally unintelligent and insensitive to continue the endless farce. As Pierre Teilhard de Chardin has written :

> Even on stacks of material energy, even under the spur of immediate fear or desire, without the *taste for life* mankind would soon stop inventing and constructing for a work it knew to be doomed in advance . . . If progress is a myth, that is to say if faced by the work involved we can say : 'What's the good of it all?' our efforts will flag.

Even on stacks of material energy, even under the spur we have the technological means to avert and control the appalling environmental threats, we can only accomplish this through a hitherto undreamed-of spirit of co-operation and personal and national selflessness. Such a sacrifice will only be forthcoming if, in Teilhard's words 'we retain that taste for life', that belief so rapidly being eroded today, that modern man is more than a 'trousered ape'; that somewhere deep inside him is something unique, call it a soul if you will, which defies all the attempts to reduce him to a remarkably aggressive and hypocritical primate. It would seem, therefore, that such an aim must become the ultimate and indeed the only logical goal of educationists and that moral education based upon theistic principles (and I am deliberately extending the term to include *all* the great religions of the world) is the only viable one to be pursued at all educational levels. Since 'theism' is a broad term and therefore open to many interpretations and misconceptions, and because Pope in *The Universal Prayer* expresses my own credo so completely and economically, I make no apology for concluding with his words:

> Father of all! in every age,
> In every clime adored,
> By saint, by savage, and by sage,
> Jehovah, Jove, or Lord!
>
> Thou Great First Cause, least understood:
> Who all my sense confined
> To know but this – that thou are good,
> And that myself am blind:
>
> Yet gave me, in this dark estate,
> To see the good from ill;
> And binding Nature fast in fate,
> Left free the human will.
>
> What conscience dictates to be done,
> Or warns me not to do,
> This, teach me more than Hell to shun,
> That, more than Heaven pursue.
>
> What blessings thy free bounty gives,
> Let me not cast away;
> For God is paid when man receives,
> To enjoy is to obey.

Yet not to earth's contracted span,
Thy goodness let be bound,
Or think thee Lord alone of man,
When thousand worlds are around :

Let not this weak, unknowing hand
Presume thy bolts to throw,
And deal damnation round the land,
On each I judge thy foe.

If I am right, thy grace impart,
Still in the right to stay;
If I am wrong, oh teach my heart
To find that better way.

Save me alike from foolish pride,
Or impious discontent,
At aught thy wisdom has denied,
Or aught thy goodness lent.

Teach me to feel another's woe,
To hide the fault I see;
That mercy I to others show,
That mercy show to me.

Mean though I am, not wholly so
Since quickened by thy breath;
Oh lead me whereso'er I go,
Through this day's life or death.

This day, be bread and peace my lot :
All else beneath the sun,
Thou know'st if best bestowed or not,
And let thy will be done.

To thee, whose temple is all space,
Whose altar, earth, sea, skies !
One chorus let all being raise !
All Nature's incense rise !

(*circa* 1715)

SELECTED BIBLIOGRAPHY

Andreski, Stanislav, *Social Sciences as Sorcery*, André Deutsch, London, 1972.

Arnold, Matthew, *Culture and Anarchy*, John Murray, London, 1962.

Barzun, Jacques, *Classic Romantic and Modern*, Doubleday, New York, 1961.

Bate, Walter Jackson, *From Classic to Romantic*, Harper & Row, New York, 1961.

Boulding, Kenneth, *The Meaning of the Twentieth Century*, Allen & Unwin, London, 1964.

Boyson, Rhodes, (ed.), *Education: Threatened Standards*, Churchill Press, London, 1972.

Brinton, Crane, *The Anatomy of Revolution*, Jonathan Cape, London, 1953.

Burke, Edmund, 'Thoughts on French Affairs', in *Three Memorials on French Affairs*, London, 1797.

Calhoun, John B., *Death Squared: The Explosive Growth and Demise of a Mouse Population*, Proc. Roy. Soc. Med., *66*, January, 1973.

Campbell, H. J., *The Pleasure Areas*, Eyre Methuen, London, 1973.

Clark, Lord, *Civilization: A Personal View*, B.B.C. Publications, London, 1969.

Conant, James, *Modern Science and Modern Man*, Columbia University Press, 1952.

Cornelius, David K., and Vincent, Edwin St. (eds.), *Cultures in Conflict: Perspectives on the Snow–Leavis Controversy*, Scott, Foresman, Chicago, 1964.

Cox, Harvey, *The Secular City*, Macmillan, New York, 1965.

Crocker, Lester G., *Jean-Jacques Rousseau*, Macmillan, London, 1968.

Dawson, Christopher, *Religion and Culture: The Gifford Lectures, 1947*, World Publishing, New York, 1965.

Ehrlich, Paul, *The Population Bomb*, Ballantine Books, New York, 1971.

Eiseley, Loren, *The Immense Journey*, Alfred A. Knopf, New York, 1971.

——*The Invisible Pyramid,* Hart-Davis, London, 1971.

Eliot, T. S., 'Religion and Literature,' in *Essays Ancient and Modern by T. S. Eliot,* New York, 1936.

Ellul, Jacques, *The Political Illusion,* Vintage Books, New York, 1967.

——*The Technological Society,* Vintage Books, New York, 1973.

——*Violence,* SCM Press, London, 1970.

Frankl, Viktor, *Man's Search for Meaning,* Hodder, London, 1963.

Frye, Northrop, *The Modern Century,* Oxford University Press, London, 1969.

Goldsmith, Edward, (ed.), 'A Blueprint for Survival', *The Ecologist,* Vol. 2, No. 1, London, 1972.

Hardy, Sir Alister, *The Divine Flame: Natural History and Religion,* Collins, London, 1966.

——*The Living Stream: Evolution and Man,* Collins, London, 1965.

Howard, John A., 'The Innovation Mirage', Rockford College, Rockford, Illinois, September, 1970.

Hubbard, Earl, *The Search Is On,* Pace Publications, Los Angeles, 1969.

Huxley, Aldous, *The Politics of Ecology: The Question of Survival,* Centre for the Study of Democratic Institutions, Santa Barbara, California, 1963.

——*Proper Studies,* Chatto, 1949.

——Julian, 'World Population', in *Scientific American,* March, 1956.

Illich, Ivan, *Deschooling Society,* Harper & Row, New York, 1971.

Koestler, Arthur, *The Ghost in the Machine,* Hutchinson, London, 1967.

Krutch, Joseph Wood, *The Modern Temper,* New York, 1956.

Laing, R. D., *The Divided Self,* Penguin, London, 1970.

Langdon-Davies, J., *Man and his Universe,* Harper & Row, New York, 1930.

Lewis, C. S., *God in the Dock: Essays on Theology and Ethics,* Eerdmans, Grand Rapids, Michigan, 1970.

Livingstone, Sir Richard, *Some Tasks for Education,* Oxford University Press, Toronto, 1946.

McNeill, William H., *The Rise of the West,* University of Chicago Press, Chicago, 1963.

Montefiore, Hugh, *Can Man Survive?,* Collins, London, 1969.

Muggeridge, Malcolm, *Chronicles of Wasted Time*, Collins, London, 1972.

Newman, John Henry, *The Idea of a University*, ed. M. J. Svaglic, Holt, Rinehart & Winston, London, 1960.

Ortega y Gasset, J., *The Modern Theme*, Harper & Row, New York, 1961.

——*The Revolt of the Masses*, Allen & Unwin, London, 1951.

Orwell, George, *Animal Farm*, Secker & Warburg, London, 1945.

——*1984*, Secker & Warburg, London, 1949.

Peacock, Thomas Love, *Headlong Hall*, Dent, London, 1969.

Pope, Alexander, *The Poems of Alexander Pope*, ed. John Butt, Yale University Press, New Haven, 1963.

Richards, I. A., *Science and Poetry*, London, 1926.

Richardson, Robin and Chapman, John, *Images of Life*, SCM, London, 1973.

Russell, Bertrand, *History of Western Philosophy*, Allen & Unwin, London, 1961.

Santayana, George, *The Genteel Tradition at Bay*, New York, 1931.

Shaw, George Bernard, 'Too True to be Good'. *The Complete Plays of Bernard Shaw*, Paul Hamlyn, London, 1965.

Skinner, B. F., *Beyond Freedom and Dignity*, Jonathan Cape, London, 1972.

——*Walden Two*, Macmillan, London, 1960.

Slaatte, Howard A., *Modern Science and the Human Situation*, Intelman Books, Santa Barbara, California, 1973.

Sorokin, Pitirim A., *The Crisis of our Age*, New York, 1943.

Tate Allen (ed.), *T. S. Eliot: The Man and His Work*, 'Remembering Eliot', Stephen Spender, Dell Publishing Co., New York, 1966.

Taylor, G. Rattray, *The Biological Time Bomb*, New American Library, New York, 1968.

——*Rethink*, Secker & Warburg, London, 1972.

Teilhard de Chardin, Pierre, *The Phenomenon of Man*, trans. Bernard Wall, Collins, London, 1959.

Tocqueville, Alexis de, *Democracy in America*, trans, G. Lawrence, Fontana, London, 1968.

Toffler, Alvin, *Future Shock*, Random House, New York, 1970.

Udall, Stewart, *1976: Agenda for Tomorrow*, Harcourt Brace Jovanovich, New York, 1972.

Van Doren, Mark, *Liberal Education*, Beacon Press, Boston, 1959.

Watt, Ian, *The Rise of the Novel*, Chatto & Windus, London, 1957.

Wellwarth, George, *The Theatre of Protest and Paradox*, New York, 1964.

White, Lynn, Jr., 'The Historical Roots of our Ecological Crisis', *The Environmental Handbook*, ed. Garrett de Bell, Ballantyne Books, New York, 1970.

Williams, Duncan, *Trousered Apes*, Churchill Press, London, 1971.

Wynne-Tyson, Jon, *The Civilised Alternative: A Pattern for Protest*, Centaur Press, Fontwell, Sussex, 1972.

Zolla, Elémire, *The Eclipse of the Intellectual*, trans. Raymond Rosenthal, Funk & Wagnells, New York, 1968.

Index

———◆———

A

Animal Farm, 27
Appert, Nicholas, 110
Appollonius of Perga, 110
Aristotle, 49
Arnold, Matthew, 33, 48, 69, 73, 121, 122
Arnold, Thomas, 48
Arrowsmith, William, 68
Auden, W. H., 41, 113n

B

Bacon, Francis, 30, 101
Bagehot, Walter, 59, 141
Bailey, Benjamin, 69
Balcony, The, 123
Barth, John, 123
Barzun, Jacques, 111
Baum, R. F., 106
Beyond Freedom and Dignity, 45
Biological Time Bomb, The, 12, 42, 43n
Blake, William, 31, 56, 74, 135
Blueprint for Survival', 'A, 66, 73n, 86n, 115n
Boulding, Kenneth, 25
Bourgeois Gentilhomme, Le, 79
Bridge on the River Kwai, 38
Brown, 'Capability', 87
Buber, Martin, 130n
Burgon, W. B., 119
Burke, Edmund, 64, 144

C

Campbell, H. J., 42n
Camus, Albert, 122, 136
Can Man Survive?, 9
Candide, 125
Canterbury Tales, 30

Chapman, John, 137n
Chapman, John Jay, 75
Chatterton-Hill, G., 57
Chaucer, Geoffrey, 30
Chesterton, G. K., 50, 141
Chronicles of Wasted Time, 41
Civilised Alternative, The, 9, 48, 92, 139
Civilisation, Lord Kenneth Clark, 33
Clark, Ronald W., 34n
Clockwork Orange, 39
Coleridge, S. T., 57
Conant, James B., 109
Cousins, Norman, 18
Cox, Harvey, 21, 26
Crisis of Our Age, The, 28n

D

Darlington, C. D., 45
Darwin, Charles, 35, 121, 122
Decline of University Independence', 'The, 112
Democritus, 34
Deserted Village, The, 63
Diderot, Denis, 31, 56
Divided Self, The, 50
Divine Flame, The, 35n
Donne, John, 30, 129
Dostoevsky, F., 47
Dover Beach, 48
Draft Horse', 'The, 126
Dryden, John, 31, 68, 70

E

Education: Threatened Standards, 69, 113
Ehrlich, Paul, 17, 95, 146

Einstein, Albert, 34n, 122
Einstein: The Life and Times, 34n
Eiseley, Loren, 25, 26n
Eliot, T. S., 20, 65n, 93, 122, 123
Ellul, Jacques, 27, 36n
Emerson, R. W., 77
Enthusiast, The, 57n
Environmental Handbook, The, 71
Epistle to Burlington, 87
Essay on Man, 25, 58n, 65, 84, 85, 89, 115, 124, 145
Essays Ancient and Modern, 93
Euclid, 60n

F

Fable of the Bees, The, 51n
Faerie Queene, The, 30
Fern Hill, 127
Fielding, Henry, 31, 123
Fishwick, Marshall, 89
Frankl, Viktor, 126
Freud, Sigmund, 92, 101, 122
Frost, Robert, 125
Frye, Northrop, 59
Future Shock, 25n, 26, 42, 110, 113, 140

G

Gasset, Ortega y, 64
Genet, Jean, 123
Genteel Tradition at Bay, The, 66
Ghost in the Machine, The, 47
Giles Goat-Boy, 123
God In The Dock, 71, 128
Goethe, J. W. 116n
Goldsmith, Oliver, 60, 63, 123
Gulliver's Travels, 43n, 44

H

Halle, Louis J., 94, 95
Hardy, Sir Alister, 35, 36, 47n
Hardy, Thomas, 21n
Headlong Hall, 61, 143
Henry, Jules, 50
History of Western Philosophy, 54

Hoffman, Abbie, 51n
Hollow Men, The, 122
Hood, Thomas, 83
Howard, John, 29, 74
Huxley, Aldous, 26, 86, 120
Huxley, Sir Julian, 16, 133n
Huxley, T. H., 45, 120, 122

I

Idea of a University, The, 74, 75, 81
Illich, Ivan, 66, 78, 144
Images of Life, 137n
Immense Journey, The, 26n
Immortality Ode, 74
In Memoriam, 32, 117

J

James, William, 134
Jarry, Alfred, 121, 123
Jaspers, Karl, 130n
Jefferson, Thomas, 21n, 72
Job, Book of, 132
Johnson Samuel, 17, 29, 30, 31, 39, 60n, 61, 88, 91, 123, 124, 134
Jung, C. G., 101, 126

K

Keats, John, 69, 129, 136, 137
Kent, William, 32, 87
Koestler, Arthur, 47
Krutch, Joseph Wood, 118, 121, 125, 129, 147
Kubrick, Stanley, 38

L

Laing, R. D., 50, 51, 52
Langdon-Davies, J., 34
Lasserre, J., 27
Leavis, F. R., 17, 44, 45, 88, 89, 102
Letters to a German Friend, 122
Lewis, C. S., 36, 52, 71, 128
Liberal Education, 99
Livingstone, Sir Richard, 24, 35n, 53, 60
Locksley Hall, 37
Loyola, St. Ignatius, 126
Lyell, Sir Charles, 122

Lyrical Ballads, 16n, 57
Lyte, F. H., 128

M

Macaulay, Rose, 122
Mackenzie, Henry, 116n
McLuhan, Marshall, 32, 41, 44, 89, 146
McNeil, William, 138
Malthus, Thomas, 16
Man and His Universe, 34
'Man in Search of Meaning', 126n
Man of Feeling, The, 116n
Mandeville, Bernard, 51n
Marcel, Gabriel, 130n
Marx, Karl, 92
Measure of Man, The, 129
Meaning of the Twentieth Century, The, 25n
Menuhin, Yehudi, 12, 19, 141
Mill, John Stuart, 39
Modern Science and Modern Man, 109n
Milton, John, 30, 51, 84, 101, 107, 135, 145
Modern Science and the Human Situation, 107
Modern Temper, The, 118, 121, 125, 129, 147
Molière, 79, 84
Montefiore, Hugh, 9, 12, 14
Morse, Samuel, 77
Mozart, W. A., 32
Muggeridge, Malcolm, 41, 85

N

Necessity of Atheism, The, 70
New Decalogue, A, 12, 14
New Impuritans', 'The, 69
Newman, Cardinal, J. H., 74, 75, 81, 95, 106, 140
1976: Agenda for Tomorrow, 115n
Nisbet, Robert, 68

O

Ode To A Nightingale, 137
Orwell, George, 27

P

Palace of Art, The, 26
Paradise Lost, 51, 52, 84, 135, 145
Pascal, B., 67
Pavlov, I. P., 122
Peacock, T. L., 61, 143
Phenomenon of Man, The, 131
Plato, 24, 34, 50, 132
Pleasure Areas, The, 42n
Point Counter-Point, 120
Political Illusion, The, 36n
Pope, Alexander, 12, 16, 24, 31, 32, 58n, 65, 84, 87, 89, 115, 124, 145, 149
Population Bomb, The, 17
Pound, Ezra, 32
Preface to Shakespeare, 29
Prometheus Unbound, 32, 108
Protagoras, 34

R

Rasselas, 61, 134
Religio Laici, 68
'Religion and Literature', 93
Republic, 50
Rethink, 9, 39, 49n, 88
Revaluation, 89
Revolt of the Masses, The, 64
Revolution For The Hell Of It, 51n
Richards, I. A., 119
Richardson, Robin, 137n
Richardson, Samuel, 31
Rise of the Novel, The, 39n
Rise of the West, The, 138
Rousseau, Jean-Jacques, 31, 51, 56
Rubin, Jerry, 23
Ruskin, John, 65, 144
Russell, Bertrand, 54
Rutherford, Sir Ernest, 44, 140

S

St. Genet, 130, 148
St. John's College Curriculum, 96 *passim*
Santayana, George, 66
Sartre, Jean-Paul, 130, 147

Savage, Richard, 31n
Sea and the Ice, The, 95
Secular City, The, 21, 118n
Shakespeare, William, 30
Shaw, G. B., 35, 86, 111
She Stoops to Conquer, 123
Shelley, P. B., 32, 70, 107
Sidney, Sir Philip, 30
Sitwell, Edith, 127
Skinner, B. F., 45, 46, 147
Slaatte, Howard, 107
Snow, Lord (C. P.), 15, 16, 44, 45, 70, 102
Some Tasks for Education, 24, 35n, 53n, 60
Songs of Experience, 74
Songs of Innocence, 74
Sorokin, Pitirim, 28
Sorrows of Young Werther, The, 116n
Spender, Stephen, 20
Spenser, Edmund, 30
State of Siege', 'The, 15
Stevenson, Adlai, 15
Stubborn Structure, The, 59
Swann, Sir Michael, 110
Swift, Jonathan, 31, 43n, 44, 88

T

Taylor, G. Rattray, 9, 12, 39, 40, 42, 43, 49, 66, 72, 88
Teilhard de Chardin, P., 39, 131, 132, 133, 134, 148
Tennyson, Alfred, Lord, 26, 32, 37, 117, 122, 130, 136, 147, 148
Theatre of Protest and Paradox, The, 32
Thomas, Dylan, 127
Thompson, J. W. M., 63
Thoughts on French Affairs, 64
Tocqueville, Alexis de, 57n

Toffler, Alvin, 25n, 26, 42, 44, 110, 113, 140
Tom Jones, 123
Too True to be Good, 86
Toynbee, Arnold, 10, 138
Traveller, The, 60
Trousered Apes, 23n, 32, 85, 123, 129, 140

U

Ubu Roi, 121
Udall, Stewart, 80, 115n
Universal Prayer, The, 149

V

Van Doren, Mark, 99
Vanity of Human Wishes, The, 91, 123, 124
Violence, 27
Voltaire, 56, 89, 125

W

Wallace, A. R., 35
Waste Land, The, 122, 123
Watt, Ian, 39n
Watteau, J. A., 32
Waugh, Evelyn, 10
Wellwarth, George, 32
Westermarck, E. A., 121
Wharton, Joseph, 57n
Wheeler, Harvey, 77
Wheeler, John A., 135
Whewell, William, 34n
White, Lynn, 57n, 71, 77, 110
Whitehead, A. N., 133
Wordsworth, William, 16n, 57, 74
Wren, Sir Christopher, 11
Wynne-Tyson, J., 9, 48, 92, 139

Y

Yeats, W. B., 22